UNDAUNTED

UNDAUNTED

SURVIVING JONESTOWN,
SUMMONING COURAGE,
AND FIGHTING BACK

JACKIE SPEIER

Published by Little A, New York
www.apub.com

Amazon, the Amazon logo, and Little A are trademarks of Amazon.com, Inc., or its affiliates.

ISBN-13: 9781503903609 (hardcover)
ISBN-10: 1503903605 (hardcover)
ISBN-13: 9781503903593 (paperback)
ISBN-10: 1503903591 (paperback)

Cover design by Jarrod Taylor
Cover photo © NICHOLAS KAMM/AFP/Getty Images
All photos, unless otherwise noted, are courtesy of Jackie Speier.

Printed in the United States of America

First edition

CONTENTS

Prologue

I was dying. It was just a matter of time. Lying behind a wheel of the airplane, bleeding out of the right side of my devastated body, I waited for the rapid shooting to stop, then said my Act of Contrition, praying by rote for forgiveness. I used what little energy I had left to finish that prayer before the lights went out.

But the lights didn't go out, and I slowly began to take stock of my situation. I was twenty-eight years old, and I was about to die. My life would never be the one I'd imagined: I'd never get married, or become the mother of a boy and a girl, or leave the world a better place, or gently pass when it was my time to go, surrounded by loved ones. Instead, my story was coming to an end on a dusty runway in the humid Guyanese jungle, thousands of miles from home. I don't know if it's possible to articulate how urgently aware you become of the fleeting nature of your existence when you're confronted with its end.

I lay there for what felt like an eternity. Somehow, through the encroaching darkness of my final thoughts, I saw my eighty-seven-year-old grandma Emma, the tough, marvelous matriarch of my family. All I could think was *I am not going to make Grandma live through my funeral. Not if I can help it.* I couldn't bear the vision of her sitting in front of my casket, suffering. If not for my reverence for her, I don't believe I would be alive today. She encouraged me to summon my will to move. Breathing heavily, I dragged my shattered body away from that wheel.

Neither my doctors nor I could explain how I physically managed it, given my state, but I pulled myself up to my feet and stumbled around to take shelter in the baggage compartment.

I survived. Survival against unfathomable odds can make every day that follows swell with a renewed sense of purpose, though not immediately, and not for everybody. But with the hindsight of forty years, I see that my baptism by gunfire guided me into the life I was meant to live: one of public service, one that would ignite the courage to make my voice heard, and one that would carry with it a visceral appreciation for each new day. That sentiment was far from my desperate thoughts at the time. Truth be told, it would have been far easier to have closed the box on Guyana long ago, or to have pushed the memory away into the recesses of my mind. What happened in that jungle was a massacre. A nightmare. Though I survived, something within me did die on that airstrip—be it my innocence or my belief in the natural fairness of life. But I can't deny how radically that nightmare molded my perspective and my instincts and how much it has informed the woman I am today.

We don't get to choose our formative moments. Very often, adversity and failure shape us more permanently than fortune and success. That has certainly been the case in my life. The major setbacks I've endured—and there have been many—have actually propelled me onward, each one reminding me how important it is to stand up again, as difficult as it may be, stronger and more steadfast. Pain yields action; it can introduce a fervor to speak out for those whose voices are not heard. Surviving Jonestown crystallized where I needed to focus my energy. It convinced me that I had a purpose. All I had to do was figure out how to fulfill it.

Chapter One

THE EARLY YEARS

Women are tough in my family. We've had to be.

My mother, a first-generation Armenian American, lost most of her extended family in the 1915 genocide. She was born in Fresno, California, where her immigrant parents struggled to pull a life together for themselves and their six children. Nancy, my mother, was the third eldest and stood in breadlines with my grandfather every Sunday to claim the food that would help feed their family. On the way home from school, she and her siblings ran from the neighborhood bullies who threw rocks at the poorer kids. Small but steely, Nancy vowed she would never be poor like that again. And because she was such a determined, self-actualizing person, she did whatever was necessary to make good on that promise.

After graduating from high school, my mother went to a typist pool for the US government in San Francisco and found clerical work at both Fort Mason and the Ferry Building. This was in the thick of the Depression—so, as the country tightened its belt, her conviction to support herself was only reinforced. Every day, she insisted on walking the forty-five minutes to and from her jobs, rather than spend the extravagant ten cents it cost to ride a streetcar. Her frugality and gritty resolve bore fruit; by the age of twenty-eight, she'd saved enough from her meager paychecks and squirrelled-away dimes to buy a pair of apartments in a gray two-story building a few miles from the Pacific Ocean, in the Inner Sunset neighborhood, where the streets are packed with a dense, blinding fog that lends the area an almost mystical feel at night. The neighborhood wasn't much older than my mother. At the end of the nineteenth century, the area consisted of miles of sand dunes and the odd roadhouse, until stretches of homes were constructed to make room for the city's growing number of immigrants and students. My mom staked her claim among them as a homeowner.

Mom quickly moved my grandmother and my aunt Tobie into the upstairs rooms to live with her. She left my grandfather, a bit of a ne'er-do-well who never provided for their family and was estranged from her mother, to fend for himself. Mom was always resourceful; her dining room doubled as her bedroom, and she rented out the rooms of the downstairs flat rather than give herself the luxury of her own space. She placed an ad in the paper, seeking boarders, and was soon contacted by a young German immigrant, Manfred Speier. He moved in a few days later. Though he was five years younger than my mom, Fred had already lived a life enriched by adventure. While Mom had been trudging up and down the same hills for a decade, he had served as a pilot in Germany, traveled through Russia, and worked as a medic in China before settling in San Francisco. As my mother was working to distance herself from her impoverished beginnings, Fred was driven by a decidedly more whimsical obsession. At the age of fifteen, he saw the musical *San Francisco*, starring Clark Gable and Spencer Tracy. Before the closing credits rolled, he'd decided that he would leave Frankfurt someday and make his home in the City by the Bay.

Fred carried with him an air of worldly knowledge that Mom lacked. By her account, she didn't even like him at first and was far from impressed, until he came upstairs one night and cooked a delicious German dinner for my aunt, my grandmother, and her. His kitchen skills and striking good looks couldn't have hurt the attraction, but my mom was more likely won over by his efficient manner and apparent work ethic. He shared how he'd docked in San Francisco on the USS *General Walter H. Gordon* without any family or connections in the area and—within three hours—secured a job flipping pancakes at Foster's Cafeteria. Neither of my parents went to college, but they were both industrious in a distinctly blue-collar fashion. Both were fluent in the value of hard work; they respected and understood each other on that level. And so began their brief and efficient courtship. On April 24, 1949, Fred and Nancy were married. For their honeymoon, they boarded a crowded train and took it all the way to dreamy Detroit to buy a car. They arrived, haggled for a brand-new Ford, and promptly drove it back across the country. Dad was charming and affable, whereas Mom was tough as nails, and likely the one who made sure they got the very best price for our car.

And then there was my grandmother on Dad's side, a woman of unwavering stamina and strength. At five foot seven or eight and 180 pounds, with wide shoulders and a mammoth presence of spirit, Emma Speier was a commanding figure. She wore a uniform of sturdy black shoes and dresses that resembled potato sacks. KGO news radio was her second religion: she was always up to speed on current events. Had she been born seventy-five years later, she might have been a member of Congress or held some prominent political role. She had an awe-inspiring, comprehensive grasp on the machinations of what was going on in the world and what it meant. She knew how to take care of business, and she knew how to take care of her own.

Grandma was a practicing Catholic, but she had chosen to marry a Jewish man, my grandfather Theodore. Their love made them outcasts in their community and country. My grandfather had served and been wounded in World War I, for which he received a medal, but in the late 1930s he was taken in by the Gestapo. As soon as Emma was informed, she went directly to the commandant at the local jail and told him about her husband's service, insisting, "You can't keep Theodore. You have no right. He cannot be here. We will leave. He cannot be here." It's never been clear to me what she had to do to free my grandpa—if money changed hands or if anyone had to be consulted. What I do know for certain is that her fearlessness, grit, and devotion got her husband released from the Gestapo. That was the kind of force that Grandma was.

The moment he was released, my grandparents got on a ship to Shanghai, where entry did not require papers or visas. They lived for years in what had become Shanghai's Jewish ghetto, where they knew nobody and had no connections. After the war they returned home, but Grandma could not bear to stay in Germany. Hitler was gone, but she saw traces of his sinister face everywhere. The wounds he had inflicted on the country and its people suffocated her. And when Grandma was unhappy, she did something about it. My grandparents emigrated to the United States in 1953, about five years after my father had arrived, and they both became US citizens shortly after. They moved into my mother's flats on Irving Street, and later to a modest home on Noriega, also in Inner Sunset.

My mom and dad were still living with her family, amid the fog of Irving Street, when I was born in May 1950, destined to take up the mantle of grit passed down from the women before me.

My memories of those gray flats in San Francisco are few and shifting; the clearest vision is of my parents, especially my mother, who was always bustling around and getting something done. Mom was petite—hovering somewhere around a hundred pounds and only reaching five feet on a good day—but she packed a wallop of a presence. She taught upholstery, with hands to prove it, as strong as they were nimble. With short, manageable rich-brown hair and dark features, she eschewed all physical adornment, refusing to take pride in her looks or attire. During their courtship, my father had pierced her ears with a pin, presumably thinking he might win her affections by gifting her a pair of earrings. But growing up, I never once saw anything fill those conspicuous holes in her lobes. She was simple in how she carried herself, in the plain dresses she made and wore, and in the manner she kept house. In reality, it was a bit of a stretch to suggest that she ever really "kept house" at all. Our home was perpetually messy, covered in scraps of fabric and cluttered with any broken oddity she was determined to fix or use for one of her myriad creative projects. Truthfully, she was what you might call a hoarder, but we didn't regard it that way back then, and instead were awed and ruled by her industrious nature.

When I was two years old and my younger brother, Eric, was just an infant, we moved to a residential neighborhood down south, right behind Sign Hill, which, in massive concrete letters, announced our neighborhood to the world: SOUTH SAN FRANCISCO THE INDUSTRIAL CITY. That house on Parkway Terrace is the first home I remember vividly. To my young eyes, it seemed positively gigantic. We had a lanai and a tiny backyard that our energetic German shepherd regularly tore up. That patch of grass was perennially shaded by the beige canopy our laundry created as it hung from our many clotheslines. When I returned to Parkway Terrace for the first time years later, I couldn't believe what a matchbox it actually was. But throughout my childhood, I was proud of our seemingly palatial home. Despite having a larger living space in which we could play, Eric and I, as we got older and more restless, found ways to entertain ourselves outside, since the atmosphere in our home was decidedly austere. We were becoming as resourceful as our mom, and one of our favorite activities was breaking boxes down flat to use as makeshift sleds to go hurtling over the steep Sign Hill of soil and dust. Cardboard-sledding resulted in the odd scrape, but it was exhilarating, and we would spend entire afternoons careening down that iconic hill.

When I got a little older, I started longing for more color in my life—which is likely what led to the first true obsession I had: Halloween. I was mesmerized by the costumes, the neighborhood houses made bright and strange with their elaborate decorations, the bountiful sacks of sweets, and the marvelous idea that everyone had a new identity, if only for that day. It was my first taste of escape and reinvention, my first inkling that thrilling worlds existed beyond my unsentimental home. Finish that off with a heaping bag full of free candy, and it was confirmed as my favorite holiday.

My kindergarten teacher, Miss Perkins, told the class that we would be allowed to wear our costumes to school on Halloween. I ran home that afternoon and convinced my mother that I absolutely had to wear my costume the very next day . . . October 30. Confused, she questioned me about it repeatedly, insisting I must have the date wrong. But I lobbied hard and was, apparently, quite convincing. "You don't want me to be the only one at school without a costume, do you?" Eventually she shrugged, pulled out the elaborate clown costume she had hand sewn for me, and made sure it was ironed and ready for the morning. And so began my training in the art of persuasion.

The next day I proudly walked myself to school in full clown attire, complete with a wig and a bright-red nose, as passersby on the street gave me curious looks. When I arrived at the playground, where everyone congregated before the school day began, none of my classmates were wearing their costumes. It was the first, but not the last, time that I let my excitement and fervor get the better of me. I ran around to the opposite entrance, which was deserted, and hid my bright, perfect costume behind the garbage cans in the playground. In the plain, unobtrusive outfit I was wearing underneath, I rejoined my class and avoided further embarrassment, until the garbage man came in to chat with Miss Perkins about an hour later. Of course, that day happened to be the one morning of the week when the trash was collected. Miss Perkins stood in front of the entire class, holding up a polka-dot garment and looking for its owner with a sharply raised brow. With no small amount of humiliation, I tentatively raised my hand and skulked up to retrieve my mom's beautiful handiwork as all my new classmates giggled around me. That embarrassment was the beginning of some rough early schooling for me. Despite that deeply mortifying moment, each year I continue to look forward to my day of revelry and masquerade.

At home, Mom was constantly accomplishing some small project, usually upholstering a chair, bench, or couch. She seemed to think that if she relaxed into a neutral gear, she would stall out. So if she found herself with a free moment, she would fill it immediately by doing things like stuffing empty tuna cans with Dacron, wrapping cardboard around the base, and covering them with little fabric bonnets—yielding a one-of-a-kind pin cushion. They were adorable, a sweet embodiment of her industrious nature. I still have five or six of them, and when I went to Armenia for the centennial of the genocide, where others laid down flowers, I left behind one of Mom's inimitable pin cushions.

If it wasn't pin cushions, she'd be creating pillows, transforming a stained tablecloth into new placemats, or crafting handmade footstools out of plywood and old cushions. On most weekends, my parents would go to the flea market in San Jose to trade some of her work. They'd also sell junk—I mean *really* useless junk, like tattered old clothes, broken stuff left over from postal auctions, or just about anything Mom could find on the street. Whatever cash they pulled in was our grocery money for the following week. They were relentless, selling their wares at the senior center or sending Eric and me out to peddle the assorted goods in our neighborhood. My parents' exceptional work ethic set the tone in our home. Both Mom and Dad always wanted us to be active, and whatever we were up to, it had to have value. Sitting and waiting at a lemonade stand would have been deemed lazy. If we wanted a nickel from our neighbors, we should be ringing their doorbells for it.

Mom often sent us into the surrounding neighborhoods to sell cacti in little containers. Though presented as beautifully as one could display a small cactus, they were still a remarkably hard sell. We'd walk up and down the streets in our neighborhood with these little clay or plastic containers hoping to find a kind soul or an easy mark. On other occasions we'd be ushered out with packets of seeds, homemade greeting cards, or any old thing Mom had crafted. What kid (or adult) wants to go door-to-door selling thirdhand wares? I never understood why we were forced to go on those missions. There wasn't a tremendous profit to be made in cacti. But we did it without questions and handed over our measly proceeds to her by the day's end. I'd like to imagine she was nudging us into the greater world as a means of cultivating confidence, not merely to bring in a dollar or two. After all, it did take some semblance of courage and audacity to enable us to knock on strangers' doors, engage them in conversation, and try to make a deal. "Are you *sure, sure, sure* you don't want this cactus? They're almost impossible to find anywhere else in the Bay Area . . ." We were pushed out the door to make a pitch or a deal, but in a positive, industrious way. Those encounters made me less hesitant with strangers and less shy with adults, for sure. Of course I underestimated those lessons at the time. The training did, however, give me a decided advantage in high school—once you've hawked cacti, selling chocolate bars is a snap.

My parents' dogged, frugal ethos meant that I did not have an upbringing of any notable extravagance. But I still had a good one. Dad was bright and optimistic, and I modeled my attitude on his. I don't remember ever minding our modest circumstances. Though we never made Christmas lists, we were always gifted *something* and were raised to be happy about it. That attitude came easy, with one notable exception: the year I received a dented suitcase from Santa (I do have a distinct memory of sulking with disappointment after receiving that gift). Gifts only went one way—parent to child—and it was unheard of for my brother or me to spend any money getting trinkets for our parents. My mother *never* went shopping for herself—she wouldn't dream of it. Everything I ever bought for her, even when I was making a decent salary, she would immediately return. The one thing I remember her keeping was a large crystal vase I bought with my tiny savings when I was thirteen years old. I was so proud to give it to her, all the more so because she didn't promptly take it to sell at the flea market the following weekend. It was on display in her home throughout her life, often filled with plastic flowers and, later, with silk ones, when crafting them became a creative outlet for me.

Eric also picked up a few lessons about frugality and hard work. He had a newspaper route, which seemed so grown-up to me. He'd ride his bike and deliver papers after school, making sure everyone on his route had access to the news of the day. It seemed an exciting, necessary service, and I was secretly delighted anytime he was sick and asked me to fill in for him. One year, he pulled in the highest number of new subscribers of all the local paperboys, which meant that he was invited to visit the San Francisco Giants' training camp in Arizona. More importantly for me, it meant I was given the responsibility of his newspaper route for an entire week. I took the job as seriously as I might have if I had been distributing lifesaving vaccines—racing all over the place on my bike, doubling back to make sure I had hit the right houses, and relishing the satisfaction of getting the job done, without forgetting a single doorstep.

Although my mother may have sent me canvassing to encourage my survival skills, she and Dad drew a hard line when I wanted to join the Girl Scouts. The uniform cost ten dollars, which they regarded as an absurd frill. I was heartbroken. Being a Scout would have meant being a part of something greater, something wholly different from the activities to which I was accustomed: they were group oriented, organized, and important. Plus, they had more interesting tasks than peddling succulents, and more exciting supplies than scavenged cardboard boxes from the local dumpster. Girl Scouts went on field trips, camped, had adventures, were based all over the country, and sold cookies—not cacti! To me, an enviable aura of unity and purpose surrounded them. But my parents would not even discuss it. Decisions in the Speier home were made without debate or ceremony.

My desire for an extended community and a bit of badge-worthy reinforcement may have had something to do with struggling through three years of being dubbed my elementary school's Queen of the Cooties. In third grade, *all* of the girls were cooties, according to the boys. But only one girl was chosen as the queen, a distinction that made me the biggest pariah of all. I'm not sure why I was chosen, but I do know that it was not a desirable election—entirely the opposite. When I walked down the hall, the boys would leap away from me and run along the row of lockers, banging them and laughing. When we played dodgeball, I was the first one they targeted. But the most humiliating event of my tenure occurred in the fifth grade, when the boys got to pick partners for the Maypole dance. I'd looked forward to the day with bright anticipation, ready to attack the choreography with gusto. Instead, I stood there with rising humiliation as each boy theatrically avoided the queen. A teacher eventually led me to the side, where I was relegated to operating the phonograph. I was crestfallen. Despite my young age, those moments left an impression on me. But they also pried open my capacity for empathy by putting me in a better position to commiserate with the lot of outcasts who, for no conceivable reason or misstep, are downgraded to sit alone with the phonograph, moving the needle for everyone else's dance.

Always eager to dance, whether at the Maypole or any other event, I turned my focus toward pleading with my parents to let me take ballet lessons. I conjured up elaborate visions of myself onstage with a swarm of graceful girls, all wearing matching pink leotards and tutus. But leotards and tutus, let alone the ballet lessons, also came with a price tag. Those dreams went the way of the Scouts; the request was met with another firm and unsentimental no.

My father wholeheartedly agreed with Mom's verdict that Girl Scouts and ballet were useless pursuits. But he was determined to imbue in me a hearty sense of self-reliance, in a way that he saw fit. He decided that, in place of spinning to no end at ballet or depending on others for team-building activities in the Scouts, he would sign me up for judo classes. Beginning in third grade, every Wednesday night, Dad sat Eric and me down and cooked us fried liver, forcing us to clean our plates because liver would make us good and strong. Then he shuttled us off to classes at Cahill's Judo Academy. I can still smell the perspiration from the old gymnasium filled with faded gray mats that perpetually reeked of saturated sweat. I stayed in judo for years, eventually completing the course offered to children. So, rather than a Scout sash with intricate badges, I earned a brown-and-white belt; and in place of delicate ballet slippers swaying from my doorknob, I had little judo trophies prominently displayed around my room. I knew the judo training was Dad's way of ensuring we would always be able to defend and take care of ourselves, but I never used my martial arts skills on the boys who bullied me, nor did I practice them on the teachers and administrators who allowed every girl in the class to be called a cootie. I wasn't a fighter—at least not a physical one. The only time I really had the opportunity to use those judo skills was decades later, on request, when I flipped Stephen Colbert—twice—after we skateboarded through the halls of the Capitol for *The Colbert Report*.

My dad wasn't really a fighter, either. He was sociable, charismatic—a happy warrior of sorts. And, notwithstanding the enforced liver, he was a spectacular cook. He made delicious dumplings and an assortment of German dishes. He'd acclimated to his new country enough that he would also cook us meatloaf, tuna noodle casserole, or fish sticks on occasion. And for very special dinners, he would make the most amazing flank steak. I remember admiring how perfectly he sliced it, and how he effortlessly maneuvered around the kitchen. One of my chores was to do the dishes, which I never minded, so long as I got to be near him. Whereas Dad knew precisely how to spice any given dish, my mother could not boil water. Literally. In her attempts to do so, she burned more pots than I can count.

My parents were opposites in more ways than their culinary skills. Mom had always regarded herself as a bit of an ugly duckling among her siblings, so she never bothered to make a fuss with her looks. Dad was tall and movie-star handsome, with an engaging smile and sparkling blue eyes that conveyed confidence. He was not a vain person, but he always took the time to comb his hair back and make sure he was dressed appropriately. Given the stark discrepancy in their height—he was over a foot taller—my parents looked ludicrous dancing together, with her head barely reaching halfway up his torso. To accommodate, Dad would crouch down, and Mom, being Mom, presumed he was mocking her. She'd get feisty and bawl him out, when in reality, he was just being kind. Our family called the two of them the Bickersons, because they were in constant snappy disagreements over nonsense. But on the important issues—the ones that usually incite quarrels in relationships—they saw eye to eye. They were always a unified front when it came to raising Eric and me, certainly in terms of finances. When it came to little details, however, they were like Mutt and Jeff, with a natural instinct for opposition; if one said the glass was half-full, the other would immediately cut in to insist that it was half-empty. They were both stubborn, opinionated, and more than willing to share those opinions with each other. Sometimes Dad would good-naturedly tease Mom that she couldn't understand something, since she had never traveled or seen the world as he had. He didn't do it in a mean-spirited way. His teasing came off as an innate antagonism, and ironically served to balance out the two of them. On the rare occasion that their squabbles heated up into a real argument, Mom's will went uncontested. No one, I mean no one, messed with her, not even my father. But there was never any question that they loved each other deeply. Somehow, using the balance of their qualities, they found a way to fulfill their American dreams—dreams defined by never needing to wait in line for charity, by working hard to contribute to their country, and by ensuring a comfortable journey for Eric and me.

The pursuit of such dreams was not an easy ride, for them or the family. I remember one time, when my father was a teamster, he went on strike. I was six or seven, and my mom told me in unusually hushed tones that Dad had to take some time off work to make things better. Things were going to be tight for a while, so we'd all have to be especially careful, she explained. I nodded slowly, not understanding what was going on, but knowing that if Dad was not going to work, it must be a big deal. That night, I waited anxiously in my room for him to come home. As soon as I heard the garage open, I ran down the stairs and peeked my head around the door. I'm not sure what I was expecting, what change I was looking for or what truth I thought I would learn from my father's face that night. I just knew he had done something both heroic and risky for the family. When he flashed me his usual charming smile from the living room that evening, it did little to lift the palpable angst in the house. I didn't know what a union was or what going on strike meant precisely, but I absorbed something from the well of anxiety my parents felt not knowing when the next paycheck would be coming.

After the strike, Dad became the shop steward, which meant that he represented the workers in negotiations and mediations with the management of his local union. He knew how to speak on behalf of his fellow laborers, an ability and status that were a source of great pride for him. My mom always wanted him to go back to school and become a doctor—she even offered many times to fund his education—but he didn't want to have anything to do with school. He just wanted to work. As a teamster for Loomis Armored Car Service, he pulled tireless hours and never complained. The combination of his fierce work ethic and the thrifty side gigs he shared with Mom allowed him to retire at fifty-five. Still, they refused to spend money on little luxuries for themselves. Instead, they invested wisely and eventually used their savings to buy a lot in South San Francisco, and then another, and then a warehouse. Over the full course of my upbringing, their nest egg grew.

You would never have guessed as much from the way we lived. After their first Ford, they only bought used cars and drove them for seven to ten years, or until the vehicles became a genuine health hazard. The furniture in our home remained the same reupholstered sofas and chairs from Parkway Terrace, save for the sundry bizarre pieces Mom picked up and renovated along the way. Everything they earned across decades of work and industriousness was put aside, should we ever need it. They always had in mind that the countless hours they clocked in were to leave their kids in good stead and provide us with the safety nets they never had.

Mom was a stoic woman; that's how she survived. She provided me with a life and opportunities for which I will always be grateful. But she was hard on me. Jagged edges leave their mark, and I knew from a young age that my instincts were less severe than my mother's. I wanted to live a more compassionate life. So I looked beyond our bare walls to study warmer role models.

I especially studied Aunt Tobie, my mother's younger sister. Aunt Tobie was everything I wanted to be: kind, gentle, loving, fun, and hip. I idolized her. She was the youngest in the family, and Mom—eight years her elder—was more like a second mother to her than a sister. In rare moments of nostalgia, my mom would lovingly recall repurposing my grandmother's dresses into little dresses for her baby sister. But, as is often the case when there are so many years between siblings, the two of them couldn't have been more different. Where Mom was reticent and disinterested in her appearance, Tobie was bold and daring with her looks; she once bleached her brown hair platinum blonde, and another time she ran an adventurous white streak through her hair, long before the creation of Cruella de Vil. Mom kept matters on staid, solid ground, while Aunt Tobie was lighthearted and silly, often signing her cards *Aunt* followed by a drawing of a toe and a bee, which never failed to make me giggle. Visits to her home were always a special treat. When my youngest cousin was born, I went over to help Tobie keep her house in order. I remember dusting all the fine china in her hutch, marveling that she had such special treasures in the glass-doored display. The little pieces seemed so precious, so exotic, so opposite to anything my mother cherished. Aunt Tobie was reliable and self-possessed like my mother, but she had a softer way of relating to others. Having her in my life made me aware that I could choose my own approach to the world, while still living up to my parents' high expectations of my character.

If Aunt Tobie modeled social grace and warmth, Grandma Speier was my spiritual lodestar. Every Sunday she would walk to church, despite the distance. When I was about seven or eight, I started listening at the weekly Mass my family attended. My father was Catholic and my mother was raised Armenian Orthodox, but they were casual church-goers. Grandma's faith was as steadfast and inspiring as everything else about her. There was nobody to whom I gravitated more strongly— I absolutely adored her. It was easy to feel drawn to someone who thought I could do no wrong, of course. But even from a young age, I recognized her strength of spirit, beyond her reverence for her grand-daughter. Curious, gutsy, and informed, she radiated the qualities my young self dreamed of possessing. She made everything an adventure. On weekend visits, she and my grandfather would take Eric and me to the zoo or Playland by the Cliff House. I adored her German cook-ing, especially her creamed spinach and Christmas stollen. For a treat, we would get to go downtown for pastries and hot chocolate. Those simple pleasures were such a big deal to me, as Mom and Dad would never consider offering such indulgences. For the Speier family, going to McDonald's was a special event that happened a couple of times a year, for a birthday or if it had been a particularly profitable weekend at the flea market. But there was more to Grandma than doting and cooking. I always saw her as a courageous and awe-inspiring fighter—the more I could emulate her, the better. She was the consummate role model in my life.

As in so many things, I began to follow my grandma's example when it came to church, attending regularly and finding great solace in the experience. I was very proud when I got my very own missal, at an earlier age than any of my peers did. If my parents couldn't make it to church one week, I would go by myself, toting my missal by my side, delighting in flipping through the thin gold-edged pages. I loved sitting in church, watching the light come through the stained-glass windows, marveling at the solemnity of the rituals. I was a studious Catholic from the start, always playing by the rules they taught in catechism. I had a little vase with a model of the Virgin Mary that I decorated with a rose crown during the month of May for the devotions. Before bed I would say my prayers and quietly say the Hail Mary for her. I felt my spirituality deeply, though I've never really known its genesis or the reason for its intensity. Grandma fostered it, but my faith was a blessing and a gift I've always had. Trusting that there is a greater plan at work has been among the most empowering and restorative pillars of my life. My faith was a profound and personal guide, one that would help me through the many terribly dark hours ahead that, carrying that personal missal proudly by my side, I couldn't begin to envision.

What did become very clear early on was that serving a greater good was my calling. But it had never occurred to me that serving others could be accomplished by *leading*, as opposed to dutifully following the scripture and sermons, until I met Mr. Edward Jex. Mr. Jex taught English and journalism at Parkway Junior High. I joined the school newspaper in seventh grade, and in eighth grade he appointed me editor in chief. For that year, I was the head of the *Panther Scream*. The responsibility, the energy, the need to stay informed, and—perhaps most of all—the fact that Mr. Jex called me Chief lit a fire, revealing a path of leadership that intrigued me. His confidence in me changed the course of my life. It was the first time that I was asked to think and make decisions not only for myself, but also for the good of a team. Being given that assignment and title gave me permission to be a leader; it made me feel that I could be trusted to achieve great things. At home, I was met with a different kind of expectation. After everything my mother had endured and sacrificed, she believed and trusted that I would do something constructive with my life, that my journey would surpass the one her life's circumstances had offered her. My dad was more specific: I'd go to Stanford and become a doctor. But Mr. Jex's encouragement made me realize that I could succeed in pursuits outside my parents' plans.

I made a few close friends in middle school, especially on the staff at the paper, and I was starting to settle into my own there, but in eighth grade I became drawn to the idea of a Catholic education. Whether it was the discipline or the anonymity that I knew would come along with a fresh environment, or a mix of both, I can't be sure. Whatever it was, midway through that year I told my parents I wanted to attend Mercy High School in the suburb of Burlingame ten miles away and an hour-long, multistop commute by bus from our home. I'm not sure what kind of an eighth-grader chooses, even begs, to go to an all-girls Catholic high school away from the only friends she knows. And given my success rate with the Scouts and ballet, I had every reason to presume that my no-frills parents would *never* let me attend Mercy. But a strong education—another luxury that neither Mom nor Dad had been given—was no pink tutu. Not only did my parents agree to send me, they sold our house in South San Francisco and moved the family to Burlingame within walking distance of the school. If I wanted to go there so badly, they decided I shouldn't have to take such a long bus ride to commute. That was my parents' way: they were not demonstrably loving, offering hugs and kisses or boxes tied up with bright bows beneath a full, gleaming Christmas tree. But if there was a way to help us achieve our goals, my parents were there to provide it.

In the thrilling confusion I felt over winning my parents' support, it was briefly lost on me that my victorious bid meant that I'd be moving farther away from my strongest champion and my matriarch, Grandma. But I would continue to see her most weekends, and I was excited to channel her courage and self-reliance. If Grandma could move across an ocean twice and rebuild her life from scratch, I could move to a new school, full of possibility. It was time to prove what I had inherited from the tough women in my family.

Chapter Two

BECOMING JACKIE

I was never a Karen—in fact, I hated my birth name. Karen struck me as a blonde-haired, blue-eyed girl. I had thick waves of dark hair, brown eyes, and dark brows, and had always favored the legacy of my Armenian heritage over my German roots. Growing up, when my mother needed me, she would almost always shriek *"Karen!"* in a tone that made me cringe. So I was thrilled to learn, while preparing for my new life at Mercy in Burlingame, that a perk to being confirmed within the Catholic Church was the opportunity to choose an additional name. Sure, the purpose was to pick a saint who inspired you— whose story resonated with your spiritual journey—but I was thirteen, and my sacrament occurred during the Camelot era of the Kennedy administration.

Like much of the country in 1963, I was wholly enamored by them. Everybody I knew, spoke to, or read about was mesmerized and uplifted by the Kennedy family, who had taken Washington, then the nation, then much of the world, by storm. No matter our party or persuasion, we were all in awe of President Kennedy and the First Lady. Initially, I was drawn in by the two of them, a young, powerful, confident pair who provoked such rapture. I was ten when JFK became our president,

and it's the first election I can clearly remember. We watched his inauguration at school, crowded around a small television and gaping at John
and Jackie as though they were royalty—or as close to it as we would
ever experience. There was an all-encompassing vitality and freshness
to the Kennedys that stirred a light of hope in millions of people, my
young self included. They were more than just a bright, beautiful young
couple; they were a bright, beautiful young couple who spoke the most
inspiring words I had ever heard.

JFK's assassination cast a pall over the entire country and affected
every American, from the youngest to the eldest. I shared in the country's devastated response—it weighed on me very heavily, as the first of
many tragedies that seemed to exist beyond reason. During that period,
I constantly sat in front of our television, a technology that had barely
come of age itself. I was so shattered by his murder that I felt compelled
to write an earnest letter of condolence to the First Lady. Months later I
received a response from Jackie Kennedy, which was franked, as it was
for federal officials. Her signature was on the top right of the envelope
in the place where a postage stamp would normally go. Jackie Kennedy
embodied a great many inspirational qualities that I believed I lacked:
grace, confidence, and national relevance, to name a few. For what
surely amounted to hours of my life, I practiced writing out *Jacqueline*,
just as it was on the letter, with her dramatic, swooping *J*. While my
mom shrieked *"Karen!"* from downstairs, I holed myself away in my
room, tracing Jacqueline's name, over and over again.

When it came time to choose my confirmation name, just months
before entering high school, I set my sights on Saint Jacqueline, who,
luckily, was an inspiration of another kind alongside the grace and confidence of *my* saint, Jackie. Known for her energy and tireless work for
the poor, Saint Jacqueline was a devout follower and friend of Saint
Francis of Assisi. She is even buried in Saint Francis's crypt.

And so, when I entered the halls of Mercy High School in September
1964, I introduced myself as Jackie. My parents didn't approve in the

slightest; they were offended, and took it as a personal affront that I was eschewing the birth name they had given me. For years Mom and Dad continued to call me Karen. But I held firmly to my decision, and eventually they accepted that I was not going to change my mind. Enabled by the anonymity of a different neighborhood and all the possibilities of a fresh identity, I journeyed into adolescence with a clean slate, one I was eager to stamp with my newly mastered, swooping *J*.

From the first day, I reveled in Mercy's environment. Religion aside, the nuns imbued in the school's culture an expectation that each student was responsible for helping other people. Their encouraging each of us to participate in society and engage in selfless tasks gave me a phenomenal grounding. Academically, I was surprised to find that I was too advanced in some of my subjects. The equal-opportunity Sisters wanted the students to be educated on a level playing field, but I had already taken the basic freshman classes like algebra and introductory Spanish, so they placed me in geometry with the older girls, which is where I met my first and best high school girlfriend, Kathleen Wentworth, who sat across from me. Each grade at Mercy had its own sweater color, so I was the only white sweater in a sea of pink. Curious why I was there, Kathleen struck up a conversation, and we hit it off immediately. I'll always be grateful for wearing the only white sweater in the class, as it launched a lifelong friendship. Kathleen was kind and direct—the type of person with whom I could be myself. She had a wicked sense of humor that made me laugh and still comforts me quite regularly, more than fifty years later.

In place of the introductory classes that I had already taken, the nuns signed me up for two periods of home economics: sewing and cooking. Even in those filler classes, I learned that I could create things, that I could execute a vision under my hands. In the sewing class, I got uncommonly excited about making my very own suit—a camel-colored wool skirt and jacket—and a blouse. The blouse and the lining of the jacket matched, which I believed was so in vogue—I mean true high fashion. I couldn't wait to get started. I made the mistake, however, of asking Mom to take me shopping for the fabric.

Whenever I visited my mother instructing her upholstery class, I had to admire what an enlivening teacher she was. The adult students flocked to her class for four decades. Some would even reupholster the same piece of furniture three years later simply because they wanted to stay in her class. But for a girl in high school picking out the material for my chic camel suit, she did not offer me much room to be creative or self-sufficient. She was right over my shoulder the whole time, yelling, "You don't need that much! No! Here, give it to me, I'll show you. You don't have to do it the way the pattern says—you can do it *this* way instead." Met with her insistence and expertise, I cowered and sulked. Admittedly, I'd seen her dole out a similar tough love to her students—she heaped it on, and they adored it, perhaps because they could escape. Her catchphrase, heard in all of her classes as she walked around the room surveying her students, was a resounding "Rip it out!" If the slightest stitch had been done incorrectly, she'd deliver her line to some unsuspecting student, much to the delight of the rest of the class. And of course, under her direction, my suit turned out perfectly, but I had been excited about accomplishing something entirely on my own. My mother's best intentions, and her need to get things done as efficiently and modestly as possible, inadvertently took the wind out of my sails. Somehow the suit lost a little of its allure by the time we were done, and I began to grasp that I needed to seek out my own brand of confidence and expertise.

Friends like Kathleen became a big part of my life, but it was the nuns who most profoundly defined my high school experience. Hardy women were the fabric of my most formative early influences, and the Sisters made up a sizable patch of it. They introduced me to an entirely different brand of religious life. Collectively, they remain one of the most socially liberal organizations I've ever encountered (no small feat, since I was raised in the Bay Area and now represent it!). Faith, to the

Mercy nuns, is less bound up with restrictions and more focused on action. They don't highlight the "shalt nots" of the Bible but instead drew attention to the positive actions. These are not nuns who quietly demur. In fact, they defy the standard perception of submissive, docile worshippers. They are feisty, outspoken women who guided me through adolescence and infused me with an unshakable commitment to public service. Their mission is to guide young women to live in the service of others, not because charity provides a passport to heaven or because punishment awaits otherwise. Their ethos is to treat others with charity, strength, and mercy, because—at the risk of oversimplification—it's the right thing to do.

Under their guidance and tenets, the environment at Mercy allowed me to develop leadership skills that I doubt would have thrived to the same extent had I been in my coed school. Attending an all-girls school gave me a surge of confidence I had yet to experience. I felt encouraged to push myself without fear of boys' judgments or their nasty nicknames that had plagued me in the past. And Mercy, with its overt focus on social justice, left little room for standard schoolyard narrow-mindedness, or the "mean girls" factor. Instead, it gave us girls a directive: we were capable of improving the world, and it was our *duty* to do so.

I was so inspired by their model of living and devotion that for a time I entertained the possibility of becoming a nun. During high school, we were offered an exploration weekend to figure out if the Sisters' way of life was our calling. It was like a retreat; we attended Mass with them and got to observe what it would mean, on a day-to-day basis, to join the order. They gave us a very authentic weekend and involved us in each of their duties and daily tasks, so we would understand the limits of their very devout, modest lifestyle. I spent a mostly sleepless night alone in a small, austere nun's room, staring at the cross that adorned the otherwise sparsely decorated wall. That weekend served as a test run to see if becoming a nun was in fact my calling.

Turned out it was not. That is not to say that I didn't give it serious consideration. There was definitely something that drew me to the ideal by which they lived. But my gut knew that I wanted to both engage in the public good that the Sisters performed and have the authority and bustling activity I'd experienced as the Chief. After accepting that I would not manifest my commitment to others in a habit, I pivoted in search of another way to serve.

I threw myself into all kinds of activities—which is to say that I signed up for a lot of them and gave them my best effort. I tried volleyball and synchronized swimming, but I wasn't especially talented at either. Kathleen and I both became cheerleaders for our all-girls school. I was never crazy about being placed on the sidelines, though, so I was thrilled to be invited to a leadership development camp at the American Red Cross at the end of my sophomore year. The classes on how best to lead had a long-lasting influence, but I was also excited about another of its benefits—namely, meeting boys. I had dated a little throughout high school, but I had never had anything resembling a relationship, given our limited access to boys. Besides, my mother was borderline puritanical about her insistence that I should never let anybody kiss me until I was sweet sixteen. That Red Cross summer, I met Paul, who gave me my first kiss at the end of a camp dance, about a month after my sixteenth birthday, satisfying Mom's admonition.

Summers at camp expanded my social life in a way that made me curious about the world around me. I didn't miss going on extended or extravagant trips away from home (given my parents' breakneck work schedules, my family did not prioritize—or really consider— taking vacations). We went on a total of three family vacations in my entire life, all of them road trips: the Seattle World's Fair in 1962 to see the Space Needle, Yosemite for a few days, and once to Tijuana and Ensenada so I could show off my high school Spanish. For that journey to Mexico, we graduated from our Studebaker truck with a shell on top to an International Travelall—a luxurious upgrade but for the fact that all four of us still slept in the car. Dad had a traveling spirit, but Mom didn't quite know what to do with herself on vacations. They took her out of her comfort zone and kept her from her work. Of course, that's the purpose of vacations, but any displacement made her anxious. Those trips didn't end up being incredibly relaxing affairs, and both my brother and I were just as content to stay close to home.

I became increasingly engaged with the Red Cross youth program's Leadership Council, which came with responsibilities and opportunities in the school year as well as the summer. I was elected president of my high school club, which made me a part of the regional chapter. At the club, we would sit in groups, stuffing Red Cross monkeys and making care packages for soldiers in Vietnam. It made up for being denied my Scouts training, because my favorite part of that group was feeling like I belonged to a greater family, a family that had a sense of purpose. During the summer of my junior year, I was a counselor at the Red Cross camp in Glen Ellen, which was how I met my prom date, a boy actually named Tom Jones. That summer I was also a camper at an interracial, interfaith camp, which I adored. Coming from what was an almost entirely white Catholic girls school, I was introduced to new cultures, races, and faiths, which broadened my understanding and exposed me to a diverse community of peers. We were just teenagers, having fun together instead of focusing on the problems of racism or xenophobia.

The Sisters insisted that empathy was a critical step toward creating lasting change, but—more urgently—they advocated for their students to be actively engaged in the effort to balance the scales of justice. Their approach, which has been reinforced by all the other major influences in my life, was that we cannot rely on others to take action. Thoughts and prayers are not enough; and neither passive witnesses nor sideline critics are the creators of real change. The nuns, deeply involved with the local community and various forms of outreach, recognized my passion for that message and encouraged me to take a more active role in our community. It was a new idea to me. At first, I committed every Sunday for the last two years of high school to being a candy striper at Peninsula Hospital, in the hope that it would help me prepare for a career in medicine. The job was demanding and rewarding, but I still craved a role that effected larger change, change I could see. Political pursuits meant little to my parents, whose relationships with politics essentially ended at casting their ballots. But I had grown desperate to understand more about the world—a motivation furthered by my weekends with Grandma, whose devotion and fervor for listening to the news was unmatched.

With Grandma's and the nuns' encouragement, I started reading the morning papers, keeping an eye out for people who were making real change. I was particularly drawn to a politician named Leo Ryan, who had been elected to the state assembly a few years before. I remembered seeing pictures of him in our local newspaper, the *South San Francisco Enterprise Journal*, when we lived in South San Francisco and he was our mayor. He was younger than most elected officials, which was evident not only from his appearance but also by the fresh energy his politics reflected. He had been a teacher by profession, but was swept into politics by the wave of the early Kennedy era. As a teacher of English and government, he had brought the Capuchino High School band to march at JFK's inauguration. That infamous call to national service in Kennedy's inaugural address stirred something in Ryan and inspired him to run for higher office. Having read about Ryan in his role as mayor and city councilman of South San Francisco, I paid special notice when my parents received a solicitation in the mail for his reelection to the state assembly my junior year. Inside was a self-addressed postcard for people who wanted to make a contribution. At sixteen years old, I'm not even sure I understood what a state assemblyman did on a day-to-day basis, but I filled out the postcard anyway, along with a note that said, *I'm in high school. I don't have any money to donate, but I'd like to volunteer.*

There are the circumstances we're dealt, and there's what we choose to do with them. Both were in my favor that afternoon. One of my parents could have opened our mailbox instead, and I know they would have promptly discarded the solicitation. The confluence of my burgeoning curiosity, the fact that I happened to check the mail that day, and whatever initiative impelled me to write down *Jackie Speier* and send in the card undoubtedly changed the course of my life.

One of my chores was to vacuum the house on Saturday mornings. I dreaded the monotonous task—made all the more pesky by the inevitable small bits of fabric and thread that would clog up the vacuum. I was drudging my way through the task a few days later when the phone rang. I picked it up, with the loud *vroooom* of the vacuum cleaner still roaring in the background. The voice on the other end asked for me, and then if I would come to an address in Millbrae to be interviewed. It was Leo Ryan's campaign manager. They were having a meeting that afternoon about ten minutes from my house. Intimidated but thrilled, I made an appointment with the man on the phone, and then turned to my mom explaining that I'd reached out to a local politician who had asked me to come to a meeting. She was likely confused by my excitement and nervous energy, but agreed to let me use the car. So I ran to my room, put on my most professional outfit, and set off to see how I could help Leo Ryan's campaign.

With no idea where I was going, I slowly drove up to the address I had been given. It was a regular house on a quiet suburban street, and I tentatively walked up and rang the doorbell. Inside was a small group of middle-aged men in suits sitting around drinking coffee and talking strategy. I realized I'd been invited to Leo Ryan's actual home. I felt another wave of intimidation, but emboldened by the fact that I had been asked to join what felt like an important gathering, I stepped into the room. A few of the men asked me questions about where I went to school and where I lived. They were throwing out a bunch of real softballs, and I was waiting for the real interview to begin when they nodded and one of the men said, "Okay, go to this address and get your outfit."

This was the midsixties. The cultural phenomenon of the British Invasion was in full swing, placing the Ryan campaign smack in the middle of Beatlemania. Along with the music, London-inspired fashion had migrated over to the States, and among those trends were go-go boots and short skirts. Leo Ryan's campaign hired me as one of a group of about eight young women, who called ourselves Ryan Girls. The outfit I had been instructed to pick up was part of the matching gear we all wore: a houndstooth bobby hat and miniskirt that landed just above my knee—a very provocative look back then!—thick black tights, a black turtleneck, and bright-white boots. We accompanied Assemblyman Ryan to shopping centers and campaign events to pass out flyers and pamphlets and speak with potential voters. Initially, I felt like a complete fish out of water among the other Ryan Girls, who were a bit older than I was, and certainly more glamorous—some had even won local beauty pageants, like Miss San Bruno. But I was so excited to be getting involved that it didn't faze me to stand out as the youngest campaigner. And if nothing else, my mother had not sewn the houndstooth miniskirt for me. I was in.

With hindsight, especially the hindsight that my career-long battle for women's rights has given me, I've thought back to my first entry into politics. The matching outfits were a ridiculous gimmick, and the role was clearly objectifying. At the time, however, none of that occurred to me. I was thrilled to be handing out literature and spreading the word for a candidate in whom I believed—and a candidate who was never anything but respectful and gracious to me. He took each of us young women seriously, asking about our thoughts on issues and taking the time to explain his policies to his captive audience. He made sure we could speak confidently on his behalf. I enjoyed politicking and felt invigorated by being a part of something that extended beyond the confines of my modest home and my classes with the nuns. I had found a group of people who cared about improving our community and *doing* something about social injustice.

At the same time that I was volunteering for Ryan, my best friend, Kathleen, was campaigning for his Republican opponent. Her position did not come with go-go boots, but we were doing a lot of the same activities for our respective candidates. It was interesting to be on separate sides of the same fight, but politics never got in the way of our friendship. If anything, having a friend who was interested in politics made it all the more refreshing and exciting. We had lively discussions about the candidates and shared our fledgling ideals. The official Ryan Girls only lasted through his campaign. Ryan was handily reelected, and Kathleen and I were both excited to have worked behind the scenes on a campaign. After the Ryan Girls disbanded, I left behind my houndstooth hat and my boots, but my fascination with politics remained.

My experience with the Red Cross and as a Ryan Girl whet my appetite to be a leader, an appetite established back when Mr. Jex first called me Chief. Unfortunately, that desire was not satiated in school elections, where I suffered my first major loss when I ran for student body president. I was up against Amy Bayley and Lorraine Welch, two top students who ended up joining the order as Sisters of Mercy after graduation. I desperately wanted the role and campaigned hard for it—stopping kids in the hallway to ask for their vote and putting out little handmade brochures. Amy won, and I was shattered by the loss, just humiliated. I stayed home from school for two days, which my mother, surprisingly, supported. I'm a "three-time loser," and that disappointment was the first of my big losses. But what I learned in the days after the results had been announced—and then time and again in my career—was that the sting of failure never lasts all that long. There's a quote that I've carried with me for decades that has been attributed to everyone from Winston Churchill to John Wooden: "Success is never final, and failure never fatal." Luckily, what felt like definitive failure, or at least a crushing blow to my ego, didn't mark the end of my political aspirations. Instead, I stopped hiding in my house and got right back to it. I was elected and served as vice president for my junior and senior classes.

The next year, when I was applying to college, I went to Assemblyman Ryan and asked for a reference. He wrote a complimentary letter about my dedication to service, which I used in my application to two universities: Stanford and the University of California at Davis, which were both within a two hours' drive from my home. At the time, none of my classmates considered colleges across the nation; we just didn't have that access or support. My parents told me the in-state colleges I should apply to—with a special emphasis on *not* applying to UC Berkeley, which was far too radical for their tastes, so those two were the only colleges I focused on. Dad still had his heart set on Stanford. Years before, when he was working as a Loomis Armored Car Service driver, he had a stop at a Wells Fargo bank that had just opened in the Stanford Barn, a shopping center and office facility near the college. My dad went right in and opened up the second account in that bank's history for me, so that when I went to Stanford they would say, "Wow, you have the number two account here?" Over the years, he got me multiple decals of the Stanford Indian (before they became the Cardinals), which I displayed underneath the glass of my bureau. I was pretty sold on Stanford being my next step—I even went to an admissions interview, thinking that would improve my chances. So when I received the rejection letter from Stanford, it came as a blow to both me and my dad, but I inherited my "get over it" attitude from him, and that's what both of us did. I accepted the decision, cleared out the decals, and tried to get excited about UC Davis.

After graduating from high school, as my friends and I were waiting for dorm assignments and freshman orientation, I worked as a counselor at that interracial, interfaith camp I had enjoyed so much the previous year. It was 1968, and the African American civil rights struggle was on high boil. Martin Luther King Jr. was assassinated a month before I graduated. Though the nuns at Mercy were fiercely pro–civil rights, our school's demographic was almost entirely white. I felt strongly about equality, but it was just a romantic notion; I had never truly engaged with people whose rights were being challenged. At the end of the camp session, I went out to dinner to celebrate with three of my fellow counselors—two boys and a girl. We were having fun, laughing, listening to music, and driving around the city—just behaving like normal teenagers—when we were pulled over by a San Francisco police officer. After briefly surveying the car, the officer instructed us to follow him to the station. It made no sense. We had done nothing wrong—we weren't even speeding. We didn't resist; we didn't even ask, "On what grounds are you taking us in?" We were both surprised and frightened. At the station, I was separated, along with the other white teenager, from our two black friends and questioned about our whereabouts and destination. Not too much time passed before we were dismissed, but we all left shaken. No charges were filed, as nothing resembling a crime had been committed, but that experience forced my eyes open just the tiniest bit to the injustices that certain groups of people have to live with in our country, and it made me angry. The only reason they pulled us over was because we were a mixed-race group. That was the beginning of my understanding that equality is not a shared privilege.

The senseless bias of that experience, though microscopic in scope, ignited a voice within me. I had long believed that it was the job of elected officials to address injustice. That night galvanized my sense of purpose, giving me a jolt of reality and pushing me that much closer to a life in politics, right before I moved into the dorms at UC Davis. I had never even visited the campus before we drove out with my boxes in the back seat. I showed up just as my roommate from Stockton came in. I was carrying a couple of boxes and dragging my dented suitcase. Debbie Panietz, on the other hand, arrived with an entire truck filled with racks for her clothes. Not a trunk. A *truck*. I'd been wearing a school uniform all these years, and my mom still made many of my clothes. It was bewildering to watch her unload that truck into our tiny dorm room, and I started to worry that I had a lot more to learn than freshman English. Despite my fears, we became fast friends. She was great fun to be around, with a sweet, affable nature, and we continued as roommates for the next three years. There were thirty girls in our dorm our freshman year, a newer concept of small dormitory housing. The dorm was surrounded by others that looked just like it, with a cafeteria at its center. I put on my freshman fifteen—if not more—by creeping down to the kitchen with my dormmates to steal cookies late at night . . . So, safe to say, I had a relatively wholesome college experience.

College was a revelation to me. It was incredibly liberating to be away from home. I regularly wrote my parents letters, but I immersed myself in the college experience. I started as a premed student, with the aim of being the doctor that my father had always expected me to become, excited to be following the calling I felt to help others in need. In biology class, I was caught up, interested, and understood the basics. But my first chemistry class was a bit of a disaster. The intro to chemistry underscored the fact that I was not destined to be an MD. I had already come to grips with the reality that I wouldn't be entering public service in a habit, and that chemistry class swiftly ruled out a doctor's coat as well; so I felt I needed to regroup quickly. I changed my major to the subject that had always appealed to me most: political science. Much as I had wanted to impress my dad and create the future he envisioned for me, I realized that nobody else could determine my passion. Ever since my job with Ryan, I'd been fascinated by the political sphere, and I was eager to dive deeper into that world.

Midway through my freshman year, Assemblyman Ryan came to campus to teach a seminar. I hadn't been in touch with him since thanking him for writing my recommendation letter, and I wasn't enrolled in the course that had invited Ryan to speak. But after his seminar, out of the twelve thousand students at UC Davis, he happened to start a conversation with one of my thirty dormmates.

"You don't know Jackie Speier, do you?" he asked. She told him that we lived in the same dorm. He said he was trying to reconnect with me and wondered if she could find me to say hello. He was meeting with all the seminar students after class at a restaurant in town, and she said she would try to bring me along. Without knowing where to find me, she took a wild guess and tried the library. I almost never studied in the library—preferring to study in the dorm, I had only sat in the library two or three times—but one of those times happened to be that night. She came right up to me and said, "Hey, Jackie. Do you know Assemblyman Leo Ryan? He's looking for you." Without a second of hesitation, I shoved my books into my bag and followed her. It was wonderful to see a familiar face. He was very kind and curious about how I was doing at UC Davis and asked what I was studying. When I told him I had just changed my major to political science, he smiled wryly. "Political science? Well, Jackie, you're not going to be able to learn much about that in a classroom," he said. "If you *really* want to learn about political science, you should come and intern in my office."

What many people call a coincidence has always felt to me like just part of the plan. And I have always trusted that it was that destined path that put my dormmate in touch with Ryan and inspired me to go to the library that evening. Those circumstances set me on a decades-long journey that brought me to the career I have today.

Chapter Three

Ryan Girl

Leo Ryan did not look or behave like your typical politician. Tall, with salt-and-pepper hair and charisma, he commanded a room. A whirlwind of presence accompanied him wherever he went. After he got your attention, he would tell you precisely what was on his mind, no matter who you were or whether or not you wanted to hear it. He took great pride in evading being pigeonholed in any one school of thought, he didn't pander, he was never evasive, and he always punched up, never down. Though he saw the big national picture, as a politician he was laser-focused on his district and willing to make any sacrifice for his constituents. He also had an acute ability to smell a rat anywhere.

Ryan's suggestion to me on that fated night at UC Davis—that I would learn far more about political science by receiving firsthand experience in his office—was entirely in step with the way he approached politics. He was iconoclastic, brash, and fearless. He had a profoundly inquisitive nature, and as a result, his politics and methods were based in "experiential legislating," which meant he chose not to rely solely on staffers or advisors (essential as they were) for information. He preferred to go out and experience the problems firsthand before he decided how to handle any issues.

After race riots roiled through much of the largely African American neighborhood of Watts, Los Angeles, Ryan briefly took a job as a substitute teacher in one of the poorest schools in the community. He wanted to have real conversations with the students, parents, and educators. What he learned from that experience found its way into legislation the following session. Then in 1970, as chairman of a committee overseeing prison reform, he had listened to inmates talk about the subhuman conditions in California prisons. So, under a pseudonym, he had himself booked, strip-searched, and incarcerated for ten days at Folsom State Prison to get an unvarnished perspective of the criminal justice system in California. He only revealed his identity when it was time to be released. A couple of the prisoners appreciated his efforts. He treated them as equals, and ideally he would help pass legislation to improve their living conditions (which he later did). They showed their gratitude and respect by giving him a chess set they had sculpted from toothpaste and toilet paper. He treasured it. He wasn't afraid of the justifiably angry community in Watts, he wasn't afraid of the inmates at Folsom, and, as he liked to say, he ate bureaucrats for lunch. He never let fear get in his way. I had nothing but respect for his methods, and plenty to learn, so that night in the restaurant, when he offered me a position interning in his office, it didn't take a lot of reflection before I leapt at the opportunity to observe him at work.

I arranged to start interning in his Sacramento office at the start of my sophomore year and would receive two units of credit for it as an independent study. I loved everything about it. I had my own little area, a kind of minioffice—a nook, to put it generously. But it was designated just for me, which felt like a thrilling affirmation. I was a professional with an office. My job was to answer all of Ryan's constituent mail. I used a Dictaphone—a cassette recorder used to tape and transcribe—which I brought with me back and forth to the Capitol. This was not a slick little recorder that I could slide into my pocket. The thing must have been about six by ten inches, and I lugged it around with me everywhere. I didn't mind in the slightest—in fact, I was quite pleased with myself for having been entrusted with it. I would dictate responses to constituent letters into the Dictaphone, then bring the machine back to the secretaries, who would type up the responses for Ryan's signature.

Sitting in my little nook, I developed a real appreciation for constituent engagement that has lasted throughout my career. That span of time was unquestionably when public service became more than a hypothetical calling. I was working on everything from the most trivial to the most urgent issues that people were facing. Some constituents had complaints, some offered compliments. Most people just needed help and hoped that Ryan could provide it. Some days I would research the lack of funding for schools in the district or the intricacies of the workers' compensation program; other times I would go into Ryan's office and we'd discuss the issues, one by one. Then there were the times that I'd read letters from people who claimed to have UFOs circling their homes. (Those were trickier situations, since there was no amount of policy research that could address their concerns . . .) But in the process of responding, I noticed that many of them were comforted just by knowing that they were being heard. I had to take each call or letter seriously and really listen in order to get to the heart of the constituent's reason for reaching out to the government. I learned how to respond with authenticity and clarity to every issue that came across my desk, and to do so in Ryan's voice.

I worked Tuesdays and Thursdays and filled the rest of my week with classes. At the end of the quarter, my final assignment was to write an analysis of the assemblyman's operation, including a description of my work and what Ryan did on a day-to-day basis. I really went to town dissecting his office and how it functioned, all the while assuming that, in order to get the best possible grade, I would have to be honest and critical—so I made sure that none of my analysis was sugarcoated. It was by no means disparaging, but if my childhood had taught me anything, it was how to deliver unvarnished constructive criticism. Assemblyman Ryan's office was efficient, but there's always room for improvement, and I used this assignment to zero in on what those improvements could be.

It *never* occurred to me that Ryan would see it. I had befriended his secretaries, Gaye and Maxine. They had gone to the trouble of doctoring a birth certificate for me, by whiting out the year on the original document and carefully changing the date, so that I could join them for drinks at the local political watering hole. We would chat and gossip in the office, and given that they were my pals, I let them see the term paper once I got it back. I had received an A minus and was pretty pleased with myself. A few days later, one of them was reading my term paper at her desk when Ryan came charging into his office on the sixth floor of the Capitol and paused to ask her what she was reading. "I want to read it," he insisted. Unsure how to deny his request, she handed it to him and he took it into his office, closing the door.

Ryan's background as an English teacher meant he knew how to write and he knew how to instruct. At Mercy, I'd learned that the bigger syllable words got you a better grade. As a result, my writing style was dreadful—overwrought and complicated to no end. The assemblyman didn't just read my paper, he wrote all over it, crossing out lines and annotating every page of the analysis with edits and comments. My paper had leveled critiques at his office, including one that he put his newsletter out too late. If he had put it out in a timely fashion, before the election, he'd have gotten the benefit of communicating with his constituents without using campaign resources. He responded on the page by writing, *Hell, I just couldn't get it out any earlier!!!*

When Maxine stopped by my desk, red-faced, and told me he was reviewing my paper, I basically started packing up my things. *Oh my God,* I thought. *I'm about to get fired. He's going to be furious.* I just cowered in my nook until he finally opened his door and strode over to my desk, brandishing the paper. He dropped it in front of me and stood there. I looked down, noting that he had crossed out the A minus and written an oversized C minus in its place.

"You don't know how to write," he declared. "I'm going to teach you how."

And he did. Over the next few months he taught me, through examples and edits, that simple, powerful words were more effective and would reach more people. His lessons informed the way I've written every letter, speech, or bill ever since.

That was only the beginning of his teachings. I credit my capacity for questioning witnesses at hearings or bureaucrats at meetings to Ryan. He modeled the proactive assertiveness I'd been learning from Grandma and my parents my whole life—you can't expect change unless you're willing to create it. He also demonstrated the same ethos I had learned from the Sisters at Mercy: public service is best delivered through action. All of my role models were prepared to be feisty when the occasion demanded it. Ryan thrived off such occasions, but he also taught me the importance of carefully listening—to the people you represent, and to your opponents. His every move was aimed at standing up for his community's best interests or his ardent beliefs, even if he had to stand alone. The experiential investigations that he took on as a legislator were neither out of character nor one-off publicity stunts, as his opponents were eager to suggest. He navigated his political life based on an ironclad moral compass and a genuine desire to help people.

He didn't fire me for writing that paper, but after that first quarter, I realized I couldn't continue interning for free. After watching my mother and father work so hard for so many years, it felt indulgent to keep a job without compensation. I told Ryan as much, thanked him for everything he had taught me, and explained that I needed to move on to a job that paid me for my hours.

"Okay," he said. "Let me see what I can do." He went directly to the Rules Committee and arranged to get me some part-time work that delivered a paycheck. It wasn't much, but it felt like a huge gesture, and the pay was enough to keep me on staff.

In Ryan's office I felt fulfilled and high off the work we were doing. By the time I was a senior, Ryan had gotten a bill passed called the Master Teacher pilot program. The program gave exceptional public-school teachers a substantial stipend for training other teachers. There were two pilot programs—one in Coronado and one in Culver City—and he put me in charge of monitoring them. I was twenty years old, and he was trusting me to fly down to San Diego, meet with superin-tendents, and develop two massive demonstration programs. I soaked everything up like a sponge; I kept late hours, came in on weekends, and devoted myself entirely to making sure I got the job done well and on time. After the pilot, the program didn't make it statewide. It was a little too ahead of its time, but it served as an empowering early experi-ence in the field for me.

If the Sisters and the Red Cross had sparked my excitement over social justice, my political judgment and acumen were honed by those years I spent observing how Ryan legislated. He and his hardworking staff treated me as a capable equal, and in that office I got to witness how politics (done right) had the potential to be the most exhilarating type of public service. I had the passion, but I still struggled to envision what role I wanted to take after graduation. I could have just continued working as a staffer for the majority of my career. But I had to drive to the state capitol on many occasions during college, and looking at that pristine, shining, cake-topper building, I couldn't help thinking it would be so incredible to work there. I still refused to allow myself to believe, in my wildest or most ambitious moments, that I could end up serving as a legislator in that magnificent building, but the dream loomed large in my mind.

After graduating and taking a job working for Ryan full-time as a legislative assistant, in the fall of 1972, I signed up for night classes at the University of the Pacific McGeorge School of Law. Doing my job well while doubling down on law school was incredibly tough. I was exhausted all of the time. One night in the office, I vented about my schedule to Ryan's girlfriend, who had graduated from McGeorge and was a lobbyist lawyer in Sacramento. Hearing my complaints, she really discouraged me from continuing law school, believing that it was a slog that ended in dismal job prospects—especially because I'd already made my way in by working for Ryan's campaign. I struggled with the decision, exhausted by hearing her advice and all the more unsure about where I belonged.

In November 1972, Ryan was elected to Congress, and I put my law degree on hold and moved to Washington with his staff to work as a legislative assistant in his Capitol office. I lived in a little apartment in Virginia with another staffer, Lynne Thompson, and spent all my time either working for Ryan or hanging out with his staff. I felt inspired working on the Hill and relieved not to have the added pressure of night law school classes, but something was still missing. I woke up one morning and thought, *Do I really want to be a hack the rest of my life?* It was interesting, fun, and challenging, but it didn't feel like a career, and I felt that I needed an advanced degree. I wanted to make the decisions that effected real change, and my job as a staffer wasn't going to satisfy me forever. I sat with it for a bit longer, then finally decided I wanted to return to law school full-time. Gaining a genuine grasp of the rules that govern our nation seemed like the most logical step toward getting a job that concerned public policy and development. So I applied to UC Hastings College of the Law, back in the Bay Area, and enrolled for seven hundred dollars per year. When I left Washington, I had no intention of returning.

Ryan supported my decision to return to California, and during that time I continued working at his district office back home—so I didn't stray far from his mentorship. We continued working on issues affecting residents, and I was able to pull my head out of the books just enough to stay energized by the power Ryan's office had to improve the everyday lives of Americans.

For the first quarter of law school, I lived with Grandma on Noriega Street, back in the Inner Sunset district of San Francisco. From her place, I took the bus to school every day, which was about a forty-five-minute ride. My hair was incredibly thick, so when I washed it, I put it in jumbo rollers, then under a special bonnet that stayed connected to a hair dryer all night. It was worth the fuss come morning, but I remember Grandma coming in one night shouting, "Jackie, you turn that off!" The contraption was loud, and it's a miracle that it didn't burn down the whole building. She had a point. But to me, it just signaled that it was past time for me to get my own place. So I did—a small apartment on Army and Castro. Shortly into the term, a fellow law student moved into my tight but convenient quarters.

In class, I was overwhelmed by the intricacies of the law. My best subject was legal writing, having had Congressman Ryan's schooling in narrative precision. Challenging as I found the courses, I stuck at it, knowing it would lay the foundation for the road ahead. I needed to know the lines of the law, so I could call out those who crossed them. And those were pretty explosive times: the women's movement, the Vietnam War, and Nixon's resignation all ignited protests outside the windows of my law school and throughout San Francisco. It felt like a time when it would be valuable to understand the boundaries we were meant to uphold.

As I studied and often passed by the protestors on the streets of San Francisco, I accrued a far greater appreciation of how the law could help advocate for people who were being mistreated. It made me all the more intent on passing the bar, despite what a slog the experience was. It felt like a marathon, and many of the classes were as taxing on my brain as chemistry had been in college.

The courses were tough and my work for the Ryan office was challenging, but I felt like I was accomplishing something important. I worked one night in the office, exhausted from class, and tried to plow through some work for Ryan. The chief of staff—who was more than twice my age—was also there. As he was leaving, he grabbed my face and kissed me, sticking his tongue down my throat. At the time, I recoiled in panic. It was a huge violation and made me feel ashamed, like everything I had been working for was erased by the inappropriate actions of this man, who was my senior. I was horrified, but beyond making sure I was never in a room alone with him again, there was nothing I could do about it. It was 1973—the term *sexual harassment* hadn't even entered the vernacular yet. I never brought the issue to Ryan or any of my superiors. I thought it was just another obstacle in my path—something I had to deal with and move on from. But I never forgot the shame I felt in that moment. I shoved the unwanted attention aside in disgust, never imagining that it would resurface nearly half a century later.

During my third year of law school, I left Congressman Ryan's office and took a job clerking for City Attorney George Agnost. It was law work and I was getting credit for it, though I didn't get paid. It was a challenging and intellectually taxing position, but I must admit I had a great time interacting with deputy city attorneys. They were almost like a group of fraternity brothers—loud, flirtatious, and confident—but at the time it was expected that men would rule the office at that volume. I was so unaware of the skewed power dynamics that I just felt lucky to be there, and I enjoyed the carousing and camaraderie.

Before long I found myself drawn to one deputy city attorney in particular. My attraction quickly grew into an infatuation. Dating had never been an exciting experience for me. In college, I had been laser focused on studying and interning for Ryan. I didn't have time for any serious romance. Then in Washington and back in San Francisco, I worked tirelessly: late into the night, Monday through Sunday. My work and law studies took all my energy, all my passion. There were lots of deserts and very few oases in my romantic life, so this deputy city attorney really knocked me over. We shared a mutual spark of attraction, which was as unexpected as it was thrilling. He was tall and clever, with an endless well of charm and a legitimately extraordinary voice. In addition to being an accomplished attorney, he was an Irish tenor, so I followed him around for months to hear him singing "Danny Boy" at all the Irish bars in the city—I mean, honestly. It was romantic, fun, and exciting, but it certainly wasn't an especially substantive connection.

Amid that romance, I willed myself through law school, got my degree, and passed the California state bar. With my clerkship over, I had to decide the next steps to building my career. The political landscape was still calling me, but I had yet to rid myself of that relentless self-doubt over running for office. After graduation, Congressman Ryan asked if I would come back and be his legislative counsel. I was surprised by the offer and felt like I owed it to him to say yes. He had given me so many opportunities throughout college and law school, and he had done so much to help me discover the passion that sent me into politics. He'd made me feel like more than a cheerleader in a skirt and go-go boots from day one—even though I looked the part. The decision to leave the Bay Area and my Danny Boy broke my heart for a flash of time, but returning to government work in Washington seemed more important.

I took all I had gleaned from law school and returned to Ryan's office in a new capacity, with more responsibility. I thought I would hold the position for a short period of time, but before long I was buying a condo in Virginia and setting down roots at the end of my second year there. I cast my lot with the whole scene surrounding my professional career in Washington. It was an exciting time. I was a lawyer, I had a great job with a member of Congress—who was also my mentor—and for the first time in my life, I felt financially secure. I started treating myself to some of the "frills" that my mother was so dead set against. In fact, I marched my way into a dance studio one day and signed myself up for adult ballet lessons. I was going to get my hands on a leotard even if it was fifteen years too late. It was very empowering for me to finally make those decisions for myself, to develop what I saw as grace after being denied the opportunity as a little girl. In my mind, and certainly in retrospect, it confirmed that I had earned my independence and was allowed to take the lead in my own life. Unfortunately, the ballet lessons were a short-lived luxury.

In March 1978, Ryan and Congressman Jim Jeffords joined a Greenpeace mission in Newfoundland to investigate and document the slaughtering of baby harp seals. I accompanied their delegation, and since Greenpeace was filming, I had to negotiate issues like getting the permits to go out on the ice floes. Ryan had introduced legislation in the House of Representatives encouraging the Canadian government to cease killing the seals. The Canadian officials were not exactly polite in response. Mounties and members of the local government glared at every turn we took to ensure that Ryan and the Americans didn't go near the ice floes to see the actual clubbing. Nonetheless, the quintessential photograph of Ryan from that congressional trip is of him lying on the ice floes, embracing baby seals. I remember the discomfort the Canadian government exhibited regarding our presence. They were outraged that we were there and didn't feel we had the cultural right to come and tell them what to do with their land or environment. They arguably had a point. Who were we to disrupt their way of living? The whole thing was a real spectacle, with indignant hunters, Greenpeace filmmakers, American congressmen, Canadian government representatives, and me, all taking helicopters to the ice floes to witness hunters brutally club shrieking days-old seals. After that trip, I remember telling myself I would never witness such violence, at such close range, ever again. There are usually thirty to forty congressional delegations (or CODELs) per year, and most of them are filled with cookie-cutter briefings and tours of programs the US government is funding. I admired

Ryan's worthy missions, but Newfoundland made me question if I shared his bottomless capacity to bear witness.

That same year, Congressman Ryan seriously considered investigating the Peoples Temple and Jim Jones for the first time. Congressman Ryan and I were walking down a hallway as he was about to go to the floor for a vote. He was opening a reading file, and the first document he read was an article from the *San Francisco Chronicle* from June 15, 1978. It was about Debbie Blakey, who had just escaped from the Guyana Peoples Temple. She was one of the first to escape and the first individual who spelled out the true nature of the experience in Guyana. A few weeks later he pointed at the article and said to me, "I want to go there and find out what is going on." That article also mentioned an acquaintance and constituent of Ryan's, Sam Houston. Sam's son had been killed near the end of 1976 in a suspicious accident at a railroad yard, one day following a taped phone conversation he'd had about wanting to leave the Peoples Temple. Ryan had known Sam and Bob Houston since he was a substitute teacher at Capuchino High School, so he felt all the more personally invested. Sam was certain that Jones had something to do with his son's death. In 1978, nearly two years later, Sam's teenage granddaughters were still living in Jonestown with their mother, and his worry about their safety had only escalated. Around the same time, a growing body of constituents, known as Concerned Relatives, had begun writing Congressman Ryan with increasing alarm about their daughters and sons who had accompanied the charismatic demagogue to his socialist paradise or "agricultural cooperative" in Guyana.

Jones had been a popular preacher in California with a robust outpost in the Bay Area, and many of our constituents had family members who had made the move with him to Guyana, where he'd promised to set up a socialist paradise. Debbie had worked as a trusted aide and the financial secretary of the Peoples Temple, but had sought asylum through the embassy in Guyana and escaped back to the Bay Area.

After reading that chilling article, Ryan and I arranged to meet Debbie Blakey during the August recess at an office in the San Francisco Financial District, where it was unlikely that she would be spotted. We spent an hour and a half with her, talking about her experience in Jonestown. For me that was one of the most significant meetings we had; it provided us with real background into the potential enormity of the problem. We listened with rising alarm as she offered a more detailed and disturbing account of her experience. She mentioned a Bay Area couple, the Stoens, who had defected and were fighting for the return of their young son, John. Debbie said the couple had gone to court to try to compel the Guyanese government to intervene and help. Jones had responded by threatening officials in Guyana that if any actions were taken to remove John, the entire Peoples Temple population would commit suicide. Later that year, Debbie continued, Jones woke the camp in the early hours of the morning. It wasn't unusual for Temple members to be awakened at dawn over the loudspeaker and summoned to the pavilion for one of his sermons. By that point, Jones's sermons were rarely about God, and were often just rants exhorting greater productivity in the fields or explaining how his enemies were plotting to invade and destroy the compound. But that dawn, Jones told his followers that they had to kill themselves to keep from being tortured by mercenaries who were preparing an ambush. Debbie acknowledged that even she had felt coerced to stand in line to drink the red liquid that was meant to kill her in a matter of minutes. When the time of their supposed deaths came and went, with everybody alive and awake, Jones announced it had just been a drill to test their loyalty, and they were sent back to their cabins.

We went on to compile similar testimonies from other Temple defectors, who corroborated reports of physical and sexual abuse, forced labor, and captivity. Jones had engineered complete authority—going as far as collecting members' social security and disability checks and determining when and how his disciples were allowed to communicate with their families. Members, many of whom were being held against their will, had to check in with the Temple guards multiple times per day. Anyone running afoul of the security detail was put in a labor camp, where they cleared jungle for the collective's farming. Repeatedly, in their interviews with Ryan and me, defectors mentioned forced participation in the mass suicide rehearsals (known as the White Night trials).

I knew Congressman Ryan well enough to know what would happen next. These weren't baby seals; these were the family members of his constituents and a former student. After conversing with Houston, Blakey, the Concerned Relatives, and the defectors, Congressman Ryan felt, I believe, that regardless of what the State Department had done or not done, he had a moral and oath-binding commitment to his constituents to personally investigate the situation, to the extent that he could. I called the State Department to discuss Ryan's anticipated trip. They briefed me, but also seemed skeptical about why the congressman would want to take the trip when everything was fine. Dick Dwyer, from the US Embassy in Guyana, had visited Jonestown a number of times and reported back that the community was thriving. So the State Department felt that Ryan was blowing matters out of proportion and assured us that there weren't any issues worth checking out. Nonetheless, if Ryan was determined to go, Chairman Clement J. Zablocki of the House International Relations Committee warned Ryan that, though Jim Jones was nothing to worry about, congressional solo trips abroad were discouraged. The State Department also made the determination that they would be unable to send a legal advisor with any delegation. I was not and am not an international law expert, and in my role as legal advisor to the congressman, I needed to be as aware as possible about any treaties that we had with Guyana or other legal issues that might play a role once we were down there.

It was a rocky start, but Ryan was convinced we needed to go. So he sought out others to join him. About three congressmen agreed to accompany him on the mission, but everyone backed out when it became questionable that we would receive the requisite permission from Jones to visit the compound. The other congressmen decided the trip would be a waste of time. Such opinions meant little to Ryan, who was never one to wait for official approval, especially when—by plenty of accounts—constituents' lives were in danger. He was willing to take the gamble that Jones would extend an invitation once we arrived. Too many families in the US were counting on him to make sure their children were safe. Of the over nine hundred members of Jones's congregation that had moved to Guyana, a fair number were elderly, and nearly a third of them were children. In the meantime, we had been told that the church had weapons, and that Jones was paranoid and quite possibly on drugs. The more Ryan heard, the more insistent he became about going.

The congressman wanted answers. No argument or threat would have been able to deter him. He knew that Jones had considerable political clout, with close ties to Democratic leaders in San Francisco, Sacramento, and even with the State Department of the Carter administration. Politically, there was nothing to gain—and everything to lose—by taking on Jim Jones, who was reportedly a live wire of the most dangerous variety. There was no telling what he'd do if confronted and challenged. Still, none of those red flags made the congressman pause or reconsider. Ryan didn't care about doing what was popular, and he didn't pay much mind to doing what others deemed safe. He cared about doing what he thought was right. Never one to accept thirdhand information or be dissuaded by hearsay, he confirmed that he was going to embark on a fact-finding—and potentially lifesaving—trip after the November election, to check on the constituents who had followed Jones into the Guyanese jungle.

Ryan assigned two of his staff to accompany him on the trip: a staff consultant from the House International Relations Committee,

Jim Schollaert, and me. He also invited members of the press and a few of the Concerned Relatives. I had read the articles. I had listened to hours of audiotape testimonies. From the start, I was extremely apprehensive about staffing the trip. In my gut, I did not feel confident that the mission was a good idea. It was hard to fathom that a man who had demonstrated such hunger for the spotlight would have moved his congregation to the middle of the remote South American jungle—removed from government regulation—unless he was conducting behavior that he didn't want observed. More importantly, we had literally hundreds of letters expressing the shared fear that there was severe mind manipulation at play in Jonestown. I certainly wasn't anticipating a warm welcome. Nonetheless, I was one of very few women who held senior staff positions in Congress at the time. In 1978, sexism was deeply entrenched in the national psyche: women in Congress represented 4 percent of the House and 3 percent of the Senate. I was concerned that if I gave in to my reluctance and let a male colleague go in my place, I'd be setting women in politics back. Or, at least, I wouldn't be advancing our cause if I stepped aside. I also knew I would be disappointed in myself if I allowed my anxieties to put a man in my seat.

Besides, Congressman Ryan assured me that there was nothing to worry about—he genuinely believed that he had some sort of protective shield around him, despite the fact that we weren't traveling with any military escort or protection. And though he was always skeptical, always questioning, he also upheld a decided faith in humanity and prized the value of meeting people on their ground. And I did have to ask myself, *When has a congressman ever been assassinated on foreign soil while on a CODEL?*

I had already accepted the assignment, but my personal misgivings remained strong, and I felt incredibly torn about the decision. I had heard the fear in the defectors' voices, and Jones's seeming paranoia about the outside world made him an unpredictable host. Impelled by my apprehension, I added language to the pending purchase agreement of my Virginia condo stating that the deal was contingent on my survival. I didn't want my parents to be saddled with my mortgage if I didn't make it back. I also put a copy of Ryan's will in my desk drawer and told some of the other staffers in the office where they could find it.

The Sunday before we left was a dark, gray day. I sat alone in my office and listened again to the hours of testimonies from Concerned Relatives and defectors. An indescribable pall weighed me down as I heard voice after voice describe Jim Jones and the world we were about to enter. I called my parents, my grandma, and my friends Kathleen and Katy. I confessed my fears to my friends, who listened patiently but told me not to worry. Katy and I had worked together the summer after high school at a company that sold vending machines, jukeboxes, and pinball machines. We used to chat on the phone at the end of most weeks, because the long-distance rates were cheapest on Sunday. I spoke to her at length about this terrible feeling I had that I just could not ignore. Finally, she said, "What are you so afraid of? You're traveling with a United States congressman to visit a commune—what do you think is going to happen?" I couldn't articulate what about it felt strange, so I said I was worried about flying over the jungle in a tiny aircraft. We laughed, and I told her I'd call when I got home. But the voices describing Jonestown kept ricocheting through my mind. I didn't share that or any of the details I'd learned about the encampment with my family. They wished me a safe trip. I hung up the phone with my parents and sat alone in my eerily quiet office. Looking out into the deepening gray, I tried without success to shake my premonition that something was going to go wrong. Just how wrong, I never could have imagined.

Chapter Four

Guyana

Born in Crete, Indiana, in 1931, Jim Jones was a self-anointed minister who created his first following at twenty-three years old. Having grown up an outcast and an underdog, he was fixated on belonging to something greater and being recognized as someone greater. Eventually, that desire spun into an obsession with controlling a flock of worshippers. He started his proselytizing outside a storefront church in Indianapolis, and by 1955 had formed the Wings of Deliverance church. Although he had no formal training as a minister and no affiliation with any organized religion, his high-octane enthusiasm and open-arms policy attracted a diverse range of followers. His church quickly grew and, as one of the first mixed-race churches in Indiana, played a part in bringing together a highly segregated Indianapolis. His original ministries emphasized the plight of marginalized individuals, and his early congregation was largely African American. The church was a model of religious progression, an anomaly in that part of the country. He used his charismatic ministries to preach his "social gospel," stating his noble intention to raise up all those who had been left on the margins of society. He attracted devotees by promoting the creation of a society in which everyone would be treated the same: a community that did not discriminate or take into account race, background, and previous circumstances.

Over the course of a decade, his congregation moved, accrued members, and changed names several times before settling on Peoples Temple around 1964. That growing community landed in Redwood Valley in Northern California. Beyond the progressive climate of the West Coast, Jones chose a remote hamlet near Ukiah, believing it was one of a few places in the country that could survive a nuclear holocaust. Always preaching promises of salvation from behind his characteristic dim glasses and slicked, dark hair, Jones insisted he was creating a heaven on earth, and he cast himself in the role of God. Much of his manipulative behavior was overlooked. Even as he began taking property, paychecks, and social security from his members, his impassioned messages and lengthy sermons spoke persuasively of creating love and equality. He assured his followers that if they joined him, they would be given health care, education, and a family who would never mistreat them.

Around 1972, after almost a decade of intensive development, Jones moved the Temple's headquarters to San Francisco. The city's reputation for welcoming the dispossessed made it the ideal urban base for Jones and his disciples. Based in his three-story building on Geary Street, the headquarters had two sets of locked doors, with guards patrolling the aisles during services and a policy of barring passersby from dropping in unannounced on Sunday mornings—despite Jones's supposed proclamation of inclusion. The tumult of the late sixties and seventies had left masses of people searching for a greater sense of security and for guidance. Though driven by the kind of underlying insecurity that so often fuels tyrants, Jones appeared to offer hope, redemption, and an idealistic new life for his members. He answered those who were seeking meaning, regardless of their race, age, or history, and bellowed back with a vision for their salvation. Should they have any doubt of his intentions, they could look to the vibrant community of believers who echoed his sentiments and treated his words as gospel.

His church was applauded for its social programs, and Jones's promises to feed the poor and take on segregation found receptive ears among San Francisco's progressive politicians. He became active in local politics, giving money, running food programs, and busing Temple members to rallies and precincts to get out the vote for his favored candidates who were running for office. He and the Peoples Temple arguably played a huge role in electing Mayor George Moscone in 1975, then again in defeating a recall attempt in 1977. Several politicians praised Jones, none more effusively than Supervisor Harvey Milk, who went as far as writing a letter to President Jimmy Carter extoling Jones's work. After the 1975 election, Mayor Moscone appointed Jones chairman of the San Francisco Housing Authority Commission, even as questions had started swirling about where, or from whom, Jones was getting his money.

By 1977, the Peoples Temple began losing members, and those ex-devotees shared stories about the darker side of the Temple and its haranguing chief. Those stories led to inquiries that would support an exposé on Jones's methods, written by Marshall Kilduff and Phil Tracy of *New West Magazine* and planned for publication in the summer of 1977. The article dissected Jones's rise, revealing his practices of manipulation, public humiliation, and fake healings. The article also clearly called out the Temple's corrupt financial structure and included ex-members' testimonies of sexual assault and brutal beatings by Jones's hand or at his command. Before going to print, the editor of the magazine, Rosalie Wright, who held some esteem for Jones, felt compelled to call him, read him the article, and tell him it was going to press. While still on the phone listening to the allegations that would soon be released to the public, Jones scribbled a note to the Temple members who were in the room with him: *We leave tonight. Notify Georgetown (Guyana).* Before the *New West* issue had even hit the stands, Jones and hundreds of his followers had left San Francisco for their promised land in Guyana, on the North Atlantic coast of South America. Many were eager to be a part of Jones's vision for their remote heaven, while Jones convinced the more hesitant among them by claiming that America was facing an imminent and devastating threat from abroad. Jones and his flock of believers settled amid the dense, isolated jungle terrain, carving out a compound that their self-proclaimed messiah quickly dubbed Jonestown.

Before our congressional delegation was set to depart, Congressman Ryan sent the following telegram, which I helped draft.

```
November 1, 1978
Reverend Jim Jones
Peoples Temple
Box 893
Mission Village (Guyana)
South America

Dear Rev. Jones,

In recent months my office has been vis-
ited by constituents who are relatives of
members of your church and who expressed
anxiety about mothers and fathers, sons
and daughters, brothers and sisters who
have elected to assist you in the devel-
opment of your church in Guyana.
```

I have listened to others who have told
me that such concerns are exaggerated.
They have been supportive of your church
and your work. Your effort, involving
so many Americans from a single United
States geographic location, is unique.
In an effort to be responsive to these
constituents with differing perspectives
and to learn more about your church and
its work, I intend to visit Guyana and
talk with appropriate government officials. I do so as a part of my assigned
responsibilities as a member of the House
Committee on International Relations.
Congressman Ed Derwinski (Republican,
Illinois), also a member of the committee, and staff members of the committee
will be accompanying me.

While we are in Guyana, I have asked
our ambassador, John Burke, to make
arrangements for transportation to visit
your church and agricultural station
at Jonestown. It goes without saying
that I am most interested in a visit to
Jonestown, and would appreciate whatever
courtesies you can extend to our congressional delegation.

Please consider this letter to be an open
and honest request to you for information about your work which has been the

center of your life and purpose for so
many years. In the interest of simplify-
ing communications, it will only be necessary for you to respond to Ambassador
John R. Burke at the American Embassy in
Georgetown. Since the details of our trip
are still being arranged, I am sure the
ambassador and his staff will be able to
keep you informed.

I look forward to talking with you either
in Jonestown or Georgetown.

Sincerely yours,
LEO J. RYAN
Member of Congress

We left Washington on November 14, 1978. When we landed in
Georgetown, Guyana's capital, shortly after midnight, we were met
by dense heat, stifling humidity, and Dick Dwyer, an embassy official
who made the atmosphere all the more oppressive with aggressive questioning that belied his anxiety about our delegation. Everybody in the
embassy had been made aware that a congressional delegation was coming to assess the situation, which put them all on edge. The mood was
contagious, a tinderbox of raw nerves that made us all apprehensive. We
stayed at the Pegasus Hotel in Georgetown. There was a little reception,
which was terribly uncomfortable, in part because there were so many
of us, but more clearly because everybody knew that we were unwanted
guests who hadn't even received an invitation to Jonestown yet.

The morning after our arrival, Congressman Ryan, Jim Schollaert,
and I attended a closed-door briefing by Ambassador John Burke and
his staff at the US Embassy. Dick Dwyer showed us a slideshow of his

visit to Jonestown from the previous May. Among the slides were a number of frames of Dwyer smiling with Jim Jones, looking unnervingly chummy. They were always standing near tables filled with food, or grinning with pride at crafts the members were making. There were frozen images of joyful children playing on swings in a playground the community had built, and slides of the bountiful crops they'd grown or exuberant church sessions that the entire community attended. It was an impressive showing in some ways, but it was also too impressive, like it had been professionally staged, like a commercial. Chief among my concerns, however, was how cozy Jones appeared to be with members of the embassy. I remember thinking, *No wonder the State Department thinks everything is fine. How could a Jonestown resident feel safe reporting any injustice to a US official who is arm in arm with Jim Jones in every image?*

Congressman Ryan shrewdly pointed out that if all of Jonestown's members were as happy and healthy as they looked in these images, surely Jones would *want* us to visit. Our suspicions grew as Ambassador Burke and his staff changed the subject and continued evading even the most basic questions regarding the Jonestown operation. They would neither confirm nor deny defectors' claims of a vastly different life inside the compound—one that included abuse and obstructed freedoms. Ryan persisted, all the more determined to visit with each indication that something didn't add up. Dwyer finally admitted that he was unable help us any further; we would have to obtain an invitation to the camp on our own. Our media companions, who were not allowed into the briefing, were anxious about being left in the dark and began asking questions as soon as we returned. I stood there as Congressman Ryan assured them that we had negotiated an invitation and would be leaving for the compound soon. That information showed up in the press and immediately caused Jones to revoke our welcome.

For three anxious days, Congressman Ryan and I, along with Dwyer and Schollaert, negotiated with Jones's representatives in their

Georgetown office. On his behalf, they repeatedly refused to sanction our visit. Each one of our baseless, illogical conversations strengthened the argument that we were sparring with a delusional madman. But the congressman made it clear that we would not be deterred, and he was not a man who would accept an inexplicable refusal without a fight. My role was to communicate Ryan's insistence, which meant I was meeting or on the phone with Jones's lawyers and disciples multiple times a day, arguing and negotiating for our invite. Finally, on the third day, we received very begrudging permission to fly to Port Kaituma, the airport nearest to the compound and about a one-hour plane ride away. That still did not guarantee us a visit to Jonestown.

On November 17, we landed at the tiny jungle airstrip. A few men, quietly exuding hostility, were standing in front of a rusty dump truck waiting to shuttle us to the compound. Congressman Ryan and I were among the first shift of the delegation to climb in for an excruciatingly slow, rugged six-mile drive to the commune. Members of the press and the Concerned Relatives waited behind on the airstrip until the dump truck could come back for a second load of people.

Thick foliage and a soaring web of wild jungle surrounded us for what seemed like an interminable journey. My first glimpse of Jonestown was of the stalks of a fresh cornfield carved out of the dense jungle, which gave way to a large clearing. The truck rumbled over the red dirt and beneath a sign that read:

WELCOME TO JONESTOWN, PEOPLES TEMPLE AGRICULTURAL PROJECT

When we reached the compound, we were met by smiling leaders of the church, including Jim Jones and his wife, Marceline. I was introduced to Jones and shook his hand. As I did so, I looked for his sideburns. One of the defectors we'd interviewed mentioned that Jones dyed them. I was eager to confirm any little thing from the testimonies we'd been given that might substantiate the veracity of the stories we were told. Sure enough, I could tell that Jones had dyed them black. I felt a brief flash of relief that we weren't on a fool's errand before fear churned within me—verifying one tiny detail could mean that the worst of the testimonies were true.

"Don't know why you're here, but we're happy to have you," Jones said. "You'll see what a wonderful place it is." He and his senior staff took us on a carefully curated tour that highlighted the aspects of the commune that put it in the best light. We saw an impressive community, with dozens of pathways, cabins, a medical center, a little school, and a large pavilion where the members congregated regularly. It was also imminently clear Jonestown was hierarchical, with the power structure resembling some sort of plantation: the majority of the Temple members were black, while the "leadership" were almost exclusively white. The presentation did not sit well with me.

At one point, Congressman Ryan interrupted our tour to make sure that the press and Concerned Relatives whom we had left at the airstrip had been given the transportation to join us. Reassured that they were on their way, we finished the tour and parked ourselves at a few picnic tables in the far corner of the pavilion area. Ryan and I asked one or two members at a time to come talk to us. We didn't want a group to present a canned response or any individual to look toward others for their answers. We worked quickly to locate and speak to the individuals whose families had contacted our office and were campaigning to get their children back home. We brought letters from those parents who couldn't join us, who feared their sons and daughters hadn't been receiving their mail. But none of the members showed any interest in receiving the correspondence from home. It was strange—I felt like I was speaking to people who had had something removed from them, like they had severed all emotional attachment to their parents and families and even identities back home. Not a single person expressed a desire to leave, not even the few who were reunited with family members who had flown all the way to Jonestown to check on them. They all swore that there was nowhere else that they wanted to be, that Jonestown was nirvana, the one and only place they could ever consider home. Each person spoke with such conviction that, individually, their insistence would have been hard to question. Listening to one after the other after the other say the same thing, however, made me feel like I was in a surreal echo chamber. They were unnervingly similar, almost scripted. It was all too choreographed. I was particularly distracted by the robotic succession of college-age girls using precisely the same phrases to gush about how they were about to get married. Larry Layton, one of Jones's closest aides and the older brother of Debbie Layton Blakey, hovered near Ryan and me. As the members spoke to us, he interjected unsolicited comments like, "We're all *very* happy here. You see the beauty of this special place." He also made a point of maligning Debbie and discrediting her statement whenever he could get a word in. Everything about him made my skin crawl.

That evening, after the second transport of press and Concerned Relatives had joined us, members performed a show on the stage they had built. Jones sat on his de facto throne positioned on the stage beneath a black sign with white letters that read, mysteriously: THOSE WHO DO NOT REMEMBER THE PAST ARE CONDEMNED TO REPEAT IT. The members were all singing and dancing and, by every appearance, seemed happy and at ease. Our dinner was plentiful, though I had no appetite and was disturbed by the fact that so few of the members were given food. Instead they milled around, making a show of how much they were enjoying the entertainment. Our group remained at a picnic table toward the back of the pavilion, observing the merriment. At the end of the evening, Congressman Ryan walked onto the stage and thanked the group, praising what they had accomplished: "This is a congressional inquiry and . . . from what I've seen, there are a lot of people here who think this is the best thing that happened in their whole life . . ." He was interrupted by the most manically enthusiastic cheering I had ever heard. It was utter pandemonium. Jones was among those who leapt to their feet to holler their approval. It went on for what felt like five minutes. Even the unflappable Ryan was visibly rattled by their excitement. It was as though they had just passed the test of fooling us and were cheering for their own hard-won victory of pretense. By the time the crowd's exultation quieted down, following multiple gestures for everybody to sit, Ryan had collected himself. "I'm sorry you can't all vote in San Mateo County," he responded with a smile.

"We can! By proxy!" Jones screamed, overexcited. "You have my vote," he added, with a little more restraint. As unsettling as I found that whole feverish exchange, there was no denying that Jonestown was a viable community, with ostensibly happy followers of every age. As I warily scanned the hundreds of smiling faces around me, I never could have fathomed that within twenty-four hours, virtually every one of those innocent people would be dead.

NBC news correspondent Don Harris was part of our delegation and well versed on the accusations against Jones. At the airstrip, while waiting to join the second round of passengers, he had spoken to a couple of Guyanese locals who confirmed rumors of assault and other atrocities at the commune. So he was especially skeptical of our surroundings. While the entertainment was still going on at high volume, Don wandered off to smoke a cigarette. A man followed him and slipped a folded piece of paper into his hand, then disappeared back into the crowd. Don put it in his pocket and took a few more steps before carefully unfolding it. It read, simply: *Vernon Gosney and Monica Bagby. Please help us get out of Jonestown.*

Soon after, Don was approached by a second member, who told him, under his breath, that we were not being shown the real Peoples Temple. He claimed that many of the members desperately wanted to leave but were too terrified to come forward. Don hung back for a moment digesting the two messages before approaching Congressman Ryan and me at the picnic table and surreptitiously passing the note to Ryan. Then he quietly relayed the sinister reality hiding beneath the well-masked song and dance.

Reading that note, I felt my stomach turn into hard knots of terror. *Oh my God, it's true; it's really true*, I thought. I didn't know what we were going to do. Suddenly, the revelry surrounding us felt menacing, and my heart started pounding. Instantly, I felt nauseated. Ryan decided that we would wait until morning to deal with it and suggested we keep a low profile until then. The media were not allowed to stay the night at Jonestown and were brought back to a hotel at Port Kaituma for the night. We had plans to see them back at the compound in the morning, but Don, frightened and perceptive, told us, "I don't know if we are coming back. There is really something up here. There is really some danger." Ryan felt the same way. Despite his proclamation onstage, and even before Don had shared the note, we could all sense the palpable tension in the air, hovering just beneath the surface. It felt like if you struck a match, the whole place would instantly explode. Ryan managed to maintain his characteristic laser focus and just kept muttering, "We have to help these people." With apprehension and fortified fear, we all split up and went to our cabins, as Jones had arranged.

I slept in a cabin with other women who were members of the Temple. There were about six of us, but we didn't exchange more than a few pleasantries before lying down. I was in a top bunk, sweating and listening as the light rain became an ominous downpour. Every drop on the tin roof, inches from my head, made me shudder. Our situation had become dangerous in a way that I had never experienced. With no sense of how we were going to maneuver through it, I barely got a wink of sleep.

The next morning, we walked out into a very different camp. The night's rain had turned the compound into a sticky, muddy swamp. I put on the sundress and entirely impractical wedge platform shoes I'd packed and went to the pavilion for breakfast. I was doing my best to maintain a smile, knowing I had to appear unruffled. I noticed an elderly, kind-faced woman stuffing pieces of bacon into her pockets, convincing me that the ample spread was a rarity, just another showpiece for the guests.

I sat down and ate quickly. After breakfast I asked to speak to Monica Bagby, one of the names on Don's note. Monica corroborated that she wanted to leave, so I escorted her quickly to gather her belongings. She had an extremely anxious demeanor, and we moved as quickly as we could. On the way to her cabin, we passed by two men standing around, scanning the scene, and she whispered to me, "Those are guards." She was clearly terrified, and I was, too. I knew we had to work quickly. She gathered her few items, and we returned to the pavilion area, where I sought out other anxious-looking members.

A woman named Edith Parks had also approached Don, after the media members had arrived from Port Kaituma. She was just frantic. He brought her over to me and said, "Jackie, I think you should talk to her." She was the matriarch of three generations of Temple members, all of whom wanted to get out. As I was taking down their names, I looked over at Don Harris, who was interviewing Jim Jones. Jones, easy to spot in a bright-red short-sleeved button-down shirt, was doing his best to keep his cool, but beads of sweat were running down his face as he licked his lips and watched over his congregation. He was still rational—things hadn't completely gone sideways yet—but his anxiety was clearly growing. By that time, it was obvious that some of his disciples were packing their things. As soon as it became clear that we would be bringing more than one or two defectors home with us, the communal facade cracked, and the mood shifted radically. Increasing numbers of people approached us about leaving. My list kept growing, and many of them—evidently frightened of the guards—wanted an escort to their cabins so they could pack quickly before we returned to the pavilion and coordinated plans for their return. With Jones's wild gaze on us, I tape-recorded affidavits of their wishes to return to the United States. I asked each of them to state their names before I said, "Do I understand you that your wish is to leave Jonestown, on this day, November 18, 1978? My name is Jackie Speier, and I'm an attorney on the staff of Congressman Leo Ryan, US government."

I was feet away from Jones, close enough to hear him trying to convince people to change their minds. When cameras were rolling, he spoke of how he loved them and how there would always be a place for them—but those declarations would be followed by thinly veiled mutters about treason and liars. He was cracking, and all I wanted to do was get out of there. Behind him, the compound had become a scene of turmoil. Traumatizing family rifts erupted on the spot, with moms and dads engaged in literal tugs-of-war with their children. Amid the chaos, I approached Jones's two attorneys who had just arrived on the scene, Mark Lane and Charles Garry. They were just standing around, looking unengaged and surveying the outbreak. I urged them to assist these families that were going through physical child custody battles. As I was speaking to them I noticed that there were suddenly guards everywhere, especially surrounding those of us trying to leave. They were unarmed, as far as I could tell, but no less intimidating—particularly to those clutching their bags, hoping to defect.

Jones wove his way through the camp, doing his best to keep up his composure as he relentlessly persuaded members not to go. He sat down with Edith Parks and other heads of families, speaking to them intently as he anxiously contorted his face. He kept repeating that he wasn't upset that they wanted to leave; it was just that they were doing it in the wrong way. Meanwhile, the names on the list of defectors continued to multiply, and we had to call Georgetown to request an extra plane. What had started as a list of two had grown to over forty people in a matter of hours. The initial crew was loading up into a large mustard-yellow dump truck, and I prepared to leave with them. Congressman Ryan insisted that he stay behind to make certain that every person who wanted to leave made it to Port Kaituma safely, and I went with the first group to help keep everyone calm and make sure the right members were accounted for.

On the truck, I felt a genuine sense of relief and even chatted with Don about what we were going to have for dinner that night in Georgetown, looking forward to the relative safety of the capital city far away from Jonestown. But when the driver started the engine and hit the gas, the truck didn't move. We were stuck in the mud, weighed down by the increase in passengers. As some men were digging us out, we heard a loud commotion from the pavilion. Moments later, Congressman Ryan emerged from a throng of people with a torn and bloodied shirt. While trying to keep the peace, he had been attacked by a member with a knife. The atmosphere had become frightening and uncontrollable; the members were too volatile for the congressman to stay. So we loaded up as many people as possible in the first truck, including Ryan. Once we were pushed out of the mud and the truck sputtered to life, we slowly drove away from Jonestown. The long and jerky ride back to Port Kaituma was grim. There were around two dozen of us crammed in the bed of the muddy truck, with at least forty would-be defectors left behind, belongings packed, waiting to escape.

The truck finally rolled onto the airstrip at Port Kaituma. I was disappointed to see that there was just one small plane waiting for us. It took about twenty minutes for the larger plane to arrive, but it felt longer than that, as tensions were running high and rising at an exponential rate. I assigned single travelers to the first, small plane in an effort to keep families together. I had noticed that Larry Layton had gotten onto the truck with us, which struck me as a glaring red flag—he was an entrenched member of the hierarchy, one of the true believers. It made no sense that he would be trying to leave Jonestown. He had on a big yellow poncho, and his eyes were set in a sullen glare, peeking out under the hood. Defectors were mumbling their concern about his presence. Amid the havoc, I told Ryan that he absolutely had to be searched before boarding, and that I didn't want him on the same plane with us. Without professional security, one of the reporters patted Layton down, missing a handgun that was hidden beneath his poncho.

While I was ushering the anxious defectors onboard, I noticed a curious Guyanese boy climb up into the plane to see what it was like, probably thinking he might get a trip to Georgetown. From the ground, I was encouraging him to get off the plane when a large red tractor-trailer rumbled onto the airstrip.

I couldn't immediately identify the deafening sound that filled the air. Everybody bolted in different directions. I saw the congressman and Don Harris dash under the airplane. I followed suit and attempted to get behind a wheel of the aircraft. As I was moving toward that wheel I watched as Congressman Ryan was shot. Blood gushed from his neck. As I tried to move toward him to stem the flow of blood, he was shot a second time and fell to the ground.

I dove to the ground behind the airplane's wheel and waited, as the onslaught of bullets thumped against the metal above me. I feigned death, staying as still as I possibly could, but the gunfire was terrible, and I found myself flinching at the sound. I kept saying to myself, "I am ready and I am willing to die. At this point I just want the gunfire to stop." During the attack, about a half-dozen men had leapt from the tractor, leveled their automatic weapons, and approached fast. Screams of shock and anguish filled the air, underscored by the rapid pounding of gunfire. The thunderous refrain was overwhelming, punctuated by the smell of burning gunpowder. I was lying on my side with my head down, feigning death, while the men were walking around shooting people at point-blank range. My body was suddenly crushed by a shocking blow to my side. It felt like a Mack truck had just sped over me.

That blow was the first of five bullets fired at me from behind, piercing my right arm, leg, and back. Indescribable pain ripped through my body, consuming me, only leaving room for a fleeting thought that I should lie still and pretend to be dead. I remained there, paralyzed by shock, for what felt like an eternity, just an eternity, but what was likely five to ten minutes.

What followed is a sequence of moments preserved in my memory. It is only by placing those moments on a well-worn reel in my mind that I've ever been able to piece together what happened on that dreadful afternoon. The chaos persisted until, abruptly, a devastating silence fell all around me. I lay completely still. I have no idea how much time passed until I very slowly turned my head and opened my eyes.

Bodies lay crumpled on the tarmac around me. There was no movement, but I thought the others might also be playing dead. Congressman Ryan's body was probably fifteen feet away from me, utterly still. I couldn't see him clearly enough to know whether or not he was breathing. I was later told that he had been shot forty-five times. It's hard to know when it became obvious that he was gone, or when I realized that the others weren't pretending. But the moment I finally looked down at my own body is locked in my mind, vivid and surreal. The whole right side of me was blown up, unrecognizable. A bone was jutting out of my right arm, and my leg was destroyed. A huge hunk of flesh had been blown off my thigh. That body—my body—was the body of a dead woman. The mind does very strange things. I felt like that part of my body was no longer a part of me. The aircraft's engine kept revving, and I thought, *My God, is this plane going to take off after all this? What is going on?* I had no idea what to do. That was the moment I said the Act of Contrition. That was the moment I resigned myself to the inevitable darkness that was waiting for me. Time passed; thoughts arrived and disappeared in a strange and surreal haze. This was my end. And this was the moment when Grandma stepped between me and the darkness.

Once I had dragged myself toward the shelter of the cargo hold, one of the reporters came from behind me and pushed me up into it. I was met by a handful of the Concerned Relatives and defectors who had survived. People were sobbing. I was bleeding profusely. The gunfire had ceased, but we had no idea if other mercenaries were on their way, or if those men with guns were somewhere nearby just waiting for their moment. The engine and tire of the plane had been shot out, so it didn't take long for us to realize we were sitting ducks in the cargo hold. The survivors dispersed into the surrounding jungle. A few kind Guyanese men carried me to a grassy patch on the side of the airstrip, where they thought I'd be safe. They unknowingly laid me down atop an anthill. I didn't have the energy to move, but, as I've said many times, you don't sweat the small stuff when you're dying. One of the reporters, Tim Reiterman or Ron Javers, lent me his recorder so that I could tape a brief farewell to my family, a sort of oral last will and testament.

Some people had managed to escape the bullets, but there were a number of other gunshot victims in perilous condition, and we were all eventually carried to a tent in what had become a military outpost for the severely wounded—I was certainly in the worst shape of the group. I suffered in that sweltering tent for what must have been several hours until, somehow, word filtered in that after Jones had released his death squad to the airstrip, he had led more than nine hundred of his flock—about a third of them children—into his White Night of death. All of those people I had just been standing beside, speaking to, sharing a cabin with. All of those children. It was impossible to cope with my pain while wrapping my brain around the fact that they had all just been murdered.

There is a sickening recording of Jones coercing his followers that day. With the camp surrounded by his armed guards, he told the members to give "the medicine"—grape Flavor Aid and Kool-Aid laced with cyanide and tranquilizers—to the children and the elderly first. Some members objected, but were shouted down by Jones and the crowd of believers. He used his last minutes to preach about how they were carrying out a revolutionary act. As I was lying in a tent seven miles away,

Sam Houston's granddaughters, Patricia and Judy, fifteen and fourteen years old, were being murdered, along with their mother, the dozens of other defectors who didn't climb into the first truck, and the rest of the Peoples Temple.

At the time, I couldn't comprehend or reconcile the magnitude of the tragedy. I could only lie there as the desperation and terror in the tent escalated. We were afraid Jones's men were on their way back to kill us. We didn't know what was true, what was real. At that stage I was resigned to accept whatever my fate would be. Not that I had much choice in the matter: had they returned, I couldn't have moved in any direction. I could only lie there while the news of the horrors that were occurring at the compound seeped in through flashes of conversation.

The carnage was inconceivable. When people refer to the Jonestown massacre as a "mass suicide," I am enraged. It was nothing of the kind. Although some of Jones's most zealous followers may have drunk the poison voluntarily, the vast majority of those people were murdered outright and against their will. Nearly three hundred children were administered the poison, with no comprehension of what it meant. That included a number of infants in the arms of their parents. Infants cannot commit suicide. The hundreds of elderly among the followers were told that if they attempted escape, they would be left in the depths of the jungle to die terrible, prolonged deaths, alone. Many members had been brainwashed into believing that Jim Jones was some sort of deity: he himself claimed he was the reincarnation of Jesus Christ. Some felt they should follow their "father" wherever he was going. Still others had bought into Jones's propaganda that the rest of the world was a threat and that armed forces were on their way to enact some greater horror on the compound.

The news at the time and the history lessons to follow usually failed to mention that a number of the Peoples Temple members were shot, several in the field between the pavilion and the jungle, clearly trying to escape. Others, who presumably refused to "drink the Kool-Aid" (a

misguided phrase I very much wish could be scrubbed from our conversations and lexicon), were injected with cyanide and other poisons.
There were piles of used syringes left behind at the scene. An eyewitness
who managed to escape the massacre described how "people who did
not cooperate were injected with poison where they sat, or were held
down and injected with poison." The precise numbers and causes of
death could never be confirmed, but this was not a mass suicide. It was
a mass murder.

After hours in the tent without medical care, I was in rough shape. Bob
Flick, an NBC News producer, brought me water and potent, 150-proof
Guyanese rum to help dull my pain. At some point, I had a vision of
Amelia Earhart, a childhood hero of mine, and I thought how strange
it was that I was going to be just like her and die in this remote jungle,
where possibly no one would ever find out what had happened. Often,
as my mind was starting to feel untethered, Bob returned to keep me
alert, engaging me in conversation, asking me questions. Many of the
survivors had rushed to the closest bar in Port Kaituma. Bob easily
could have stayed with them. It was a remarkably compassionate act on
his part to check in on me every few hours and offer me rum, dull my
suffering. I will forever be grateful to him for that kindness.

Twelve hours had passed as I lay teetering on death's precipice when
a light switch was turned on inside me. I realized that the simple fact
that I knew I was dying was proof that I was, indeed, still alive. I just
needed to hang on. Maybe it was the rum. Maybe it was the encouraging words. But I lay in that state, alternating between a strange lucidity
and an utter haze. Until we're tested, we never know how much we
can handle. That day taught me that each of us is capable of far more
than we might imagine. And, as time went on and I was still drawing
breath, I started thinking about what might happen if I survived. Just

as solemnly as I had said the Act of Contrition, I vowed that if I got out of there alive, I would make every day count, I would live as fully as possible, and I would devote my life to public service.

The Guyanese army arrived by train at about five in the morning to secure the area—unsure whether or not they'd be ambushed, they had established that a train would be the safest way to reach us. The medic came over to assess my situation, and I was flooded with gratitude. I assumed my prayers had been answered, that help had arrived. The medic lifted up the tarp covering my body, looked at my wounds, put the tarp back over me, and gave me two aspirin. I gasped as I watched him walk away. It felt like a terrible joke—I couldn't count on anyone to save me. I took one of the aspirin. With no sense of how long it would be until I received proper medical care, I saved the other for when the pain became impossible to bear. There were moments when I was delirious enough to believe that whatever was going on below the tarp with my leg could just be put in a cast, if medical attention ever arrived. I had no idea what lay ahead of me.

Several hours later, I heard the groan of a plane's engine. I was carried out of the tent, past dead bodies, and aboard a chartered Guyanese cargo plane. It had been almost twenty-two hours since the ambush, and the plane was our only way out of Port Kaituma. In the unending turbulence, every bump or air pocket we hit sent an arrow of pain through my body. The plane touched down at the airport in Georgetown, where a US Air Force medevac plane was waiting. As I was transferred onto a gurney, I was terribly weak and not in my right mind, but conscious enough to feel certain that neither my body nor my mind could bear another flight. I looked up through the haze of my fragile consciousness and saw a big, gleaming white plane with *The United States of America* written on the side. The vision gave me a surge of hope and adrenaline. I felt as though someone had just wrapped me in the American flag. Every time I sing our national anthem or recite the Pledge of Allegiance, my mind flashes back to the monumental relief and gratitude I felt for being an American. Despite having lost an astonishing amount of blood, the sight of that plane revitalized my will. That was the last moment I remember with any real clarity, before I surrendered my body to the capable crew.

Luckily for me, Senior Master Sergeant Doug Benson was on the plane that took us from Georgetown, and he immediately got to work cleaning my wounds. Once we were airborne, one of the medical technicians evaluated my injuries.

"She has another three minutes," Ron Javers heard them say as they assessed my condition. We were in flight for several hours as I drifted in and out of consciousness, fighting to keep the lights on. Three minutes to live. My body and vitals were so unstable that the pilots nearly landed the plane in Puerto Rico, then again in New Orleans, for emergency triage. I didn't know how much longer I could hold on. Sergeant Benson made the call to chance it and get us directly to Andrews Air Force Base.

A few years ago, I had the privilege of speaking with Sergeant Benson and finally thanked him properly. "You had a gunshot wound in your leg the size of a football," he told me. "You were in real bad condition." When we were on the plane, he continued, I had looked up at him and said, "Will I ever dance again?" I've asked myself the same question countless times since.

"Yes. Yes, you will," Sergeant Benson answered. "And I want the first dance."

Chapter Five

Recovery and Renewal

I've shared my Guyana story countless times, but it's still a challenge to go back and relive those days, to return to the oppressively humid jungle and describe what it felt like lying on the tarmac. It's never easy to go back to the gunshots. To the stretchers. To the volatile flight home. As far as rational outcomes go, it's unfathomable that I landed back in the United States at all. Piecing the parts together—the gunshots, the bleeding, the twenty-two hours without medical care—I can't help asking myself, *Why didn't I die?* There was every likelihood that I would have. Biologically, I should have: the entire area surrounding my femoral artery was blown up. Had one of those five bullets pierced the artery, I could have bled out in as little as ninety seconds. Did I survive because of that kind of luck, coupled with a ferocious will to live; or was it part of a greater plan? I've come to believe that it's primarily the latter. It wasn't my time to die. I've tortured myself with how I did not immediately register the blessing or the responsibility that had been bestowed upon me. Before any reconciliation could occur, I had to deal with the gangrene.

As soon as we landed at Andrews, I was taken by gurney into emergency surgery. Gas gangrene—essentially the death of body tissue, caused by bacterial infection—had spread into my leg and arm. But we had made it back, and I was alive. Amid the chaos of my memories from those near-death hours, the sight I remember most clearly is my mother, waiting for me. I was overcome by relief; my heart swelled with a sense of comfort and reassurance. *I'm not alone anymore,* I thought. *I don't have to fend for myself.* Seeing her face was one of the greatest gifts of my life.

After that initial reassurance swept over me, however, I wouldn't say that my mother served as the most calming presence. I had never seen her look so pained. She was an absolute wreck—my family and friends had been receiving their information from the radio and television, so they didn't know what was happening and were terrified. The media was broadcasting all sorts of vague and contradictory information. Without confirmed intelligence to share, or because they didn't want to deal with family and face the inevitable, unanswerable questions, the State Department had never communicated with my parents. My mom could not handle the intensity; between taking her very first plane ride and the torn-up state I was in, any sense of stability she'd been clinging to was rattled loose. My dear friend Katy, whom I called just before I left for Guyana, had brought my mom to Andrews. On the night of the eighteenth—the day I was shot—she saw the ticker on the television say something had gone wrong on the congressman's visit to Jonestown. She still lived in San Francisco, so she drove right over to my parents' home and sat up all night with Dad watching television. My roommate from Washington called them with updates. And when word came through that I had gotten out alive, Katy told my dad that she was going to fly to Washington. The next morning, as she was packing up her bag, Dad called her and said that my mom wanted to come with her. After arriving at Andrews, which is laid out more like canvas cubicles than a typical hospital, Mom and Katy were taken aside and debriefed on my injuries. After performing several hours of surgery on me and debating whether or not to amputate my limbs, the doctors determined that

I needed to be rushed to the Baltimore Shock Trauma Center. They prepared me for the transfer.

When Katy approached me, apparently the first thing I said was, "What are you doing here?" as though it were just some strange coincidence. She stayed with me until a nurse asked me if I wanted to take a helicopter to the Trauma Center. After the jarring Guyanese plane ride from Port Kaituma to Georgetown, I could practically feel the excruciating bumps of the journey all over again. Certain that another flight of any kind would kill me, I made my first cognizant decision in recovery and vehemently shook my head no. So I took an ambulance, with Mom and Katy behind us. We sped through the night for about forty-five minutes while I focused all of my energy on keeping myself alive. I just had to get through one minute, followed by the next, then the next.

The Shock Trauma Center had blinding bright lights that made it feel like I was constantly in an operating room. Exceptional doctors and nurses went to work on me, clustered around my gurney. If I knew their names I would list each one of them here for the incredible work they did to help save my life. At the time, however, all I registered were those glaring lights. When I squeezed my eyes shut I had to fight a different type of nightmare: a cacophony of beeps and doctors' orders played over the memory of those thunderous bullets in Guyana. The disquieting bustle around me grew more acute and disturbing as my shock began to thaw, drip by drip. I had a number of IVs attached to the left side of my body, and I focused on them, looking up at one of the bags of blue liquid. In my delirious state, I called one of the nurses over and asked, "How many calories are in that bag?" I nodded toward the fluids that were saving my life.

"Three thousand," she responded.

Three thousand? I'm going to get so fat! I thought as discussions flew around me about whether or not they needed to cut off my leg.

Because the doctors' surgical efforts at stemming the gangrene had been unsuccessful, hyperbaric chamber treatments were the last resort.

A 1978 hyperbaric chamber—a tube filled with antibacterial microbes and high levels of oxygen—resembled an iron lung. They moved me onto a cold steel gurney, then wheeled me into the enclosed tunnel. It was incredibly painful, but I had to repeat that treatment twice a day, for several days. Every time I was wheeled in, it felt like a new test of physical endurance. Without fail, whenever I exited the chamber dive, I heaved up bile. But I also remember flashes of feeling unspeakably grateful; I was alive, and all of those doctors and nurses were there, doing their best to keep it that way.

Within a day or two, my brother, Eric, made the journey out from Seattle, where he was living at the time. So much immediate work needed to be done on my body that nobody had washed my hair yet when he arrived, and I could scarcely move. The red dirt of Guyana was still caked on me. Eric took the time to wash my thick hair clean, very gently scrubbing away all of the solidified mud that had come from the dusty air and the soaked ground. Somehow he just understood that I wanted all remnants of the experience out of my life, or out of my hair, as it was. I will forever remember his sweet gesture of love.

Given the treatments, the tension, and those bright lights, the Trauma Center was tough on everyone. My family and friends were there, but I was beyond exhausted, trying my best to believe I would make a full recovery, reeling at what I'd endured, and being entirely unsure what the next day would bring. Katy later told me that while I was in one of my many treatments, she, my mother, and my brother visited the hospital psychologist who specialized in family counseling. Mom—who had a controlling personality at the most serene of times—was driving everybody crazy. Her version of coping included pacing rooms and halls with no apparent route or destination. Though I'd lost my sense of time, I remember her shouting at the medical staff who were attempting to calm her down. It was obvious to everyone that she was too emotional to stay and wait out all the surgeries that needed to be performed. Even the psychologist, who was initially very sensitive to my mother's position, came around. She first told Katy and Eric, "You know, it's her daughter. And Jackie's received so much relief from having her here; she's her sense of security . . ." And she was right, Mom *had* brought me immense relief: that initial sight of her was one of the greatest moments of comfort in my life. After that, however, I lost focus for days and wasn't aware of what was happening around me. The day after their initial meeting, the psychologist came to visit my area, where my mom was vehemently insisting things like, "She needs yogurt! She needs yogurt!" to the nurses who were busy dressing my wounds. The psychologist reconvened with Katy and Eric and admitted that they'd been right and she should probably go home. Mom accepted the decision, but insisted that she take a bus instead of a plane. With no small measure of her own relief, Katy drove Mom to the bus station and wished her a safe three-day journey back to California.

The excruciating limb-saving process continued for nearly a week, which is roughly how long it took for me to regain full consciousness and begin to comprehend the trauma I had been through. After one of the treatments, as I was being wheeled out, a surgeon approached me with a somber look on his face. I presumed it was bad news about my condition, but after my nausea passed, he said, "I hate to tell you this, but I thought you'd want to know. George Moscone [the mayor of San Francisco] and Harvey Milk [County Board of Supervisors member] have just been assassinated. They believe the assailant was former Supervisor Dan White." I couldn't understand. *What is happening?* I had just emerged from a hyperbaric chamber. It had been ten days since I had been shot. Congressman Ryan was dead. Don Harris was dead. Bob Brown and Greg Robinson, the rugged cameraman and talented photographer who had come as part of the delegation, were dead. Nearly a thousand other men, women, and children whom I had spent a day with, witnessing them enjoying music and conversation, had been poisoned. And now, my hometown mayor and Supervisor Milk had been assassinated. I felt like the world was ending. I just kept trying to hold on as I—once again—prepared for the lights to go out at any moment.

A couple of days after that, the doctors had managed to stem the gangrene, and I was ready to be transferred to the hospital, where I would spend the following six weeks of recovery. I felt reinforced and encouraged by the impending move away from the Trauma Center, and did my best to hurriedly thank as many people as I could as I was loaded back into an ambulance and taken to Virginia Hospital Center in Arlington, about an hour away. There I had a private room, which felt like a gift from God. Though I was completely immobile, lying helplessly on the starchy sheets of a cold hospital bed, it was the very vision of serenity compared to the constant blinding glare and incessant beeps of the ICU in the Trauma Center.

In Arlington, twenty-four-hour US Marshals Service protection was assigned to me because they had been receiving threats on my life from surviving members of the Peoples Temple. They also visited the staff at Congressman Ryan's office. A threat assessment was done, which is why the US Marshals were dispatched to keep me safe. My guards were a small rotation of wonderful women, armed but in plain clothes, who helped me get by in every sense, keeping guard over my life but also providing crucial company while I was in various states of recovery. Whenever I appeared agitated or couldn't sleep, the marshal on duty would rub my feet and strike up conversations to calm me down. They were gentle but formidable guardians who made me feel safe and human in a time when little seemed certain.

Which is not to say I didn't have company—I was far from alone. There was a glass wall between me and the nurses' station, so they could also observe me at all times. My Washington roommate, Lynne, continued to check in on me as regularly as possible. Before I left the Trauma Center, Katy had flown back to the Bay Area, but Kathleen, my geometry class compatriot from Mercy, arrived to check in on me. She had just become a United Airlines pilot, Second Officer Wentworth, and had shown up in her work uniform. It was bizarre to see people who were inhabiting the real world, just getting on with their everyday lives. Having lost a sense of what my life might look like if I survived, getting a visual reminder of an existence that included getting out of bed, putting on a uniform or business clothes, and heading to work seemed unfathomable. I couldn't yet imagine that I would ever get back to that state of normalcy.

Once I was strong enough to endure it, the doctors and nurses began reconstructing my body. They performed several experimental surgeries to try to make me whole again. The biggest concern was the huge open wound on my leg. They attempted to graft pig skin onto it to see if that would suffice as a permanent Band-Aid of sorts, but my body rejected it. With no other choice, they ultimately ended up taking three large strips of skin from my left leg. They were about two inches wide and eight inches long, and left my uninjured thigh scarred and deformed. They used them as grafts to seal up my right leg as much as possible, then took advantage of human skin's elasticity to pull mine up enough over the wound to secure the strips. It was deeply painful, and it wasn't pretty, but this was not a time to be concerned about the aesthetics. With a viable solution to my right leg in progress, they moved on to addressing my right arm. In order to keep the bone in place to heal properly, they inserted steel dowels, metal bars, and pins. During the repair, they discovered that my radial nerve was severely damaged, and after that surgery, the doctor warned me that I might never be able to use my wrist again. At that stage, I was unable to lift my fingers. But even something like the use of my hand was pretty far from my immediate concerns. I was still struggling to stay alive. Just trying to stay alive.

Any time I had a moment and the wherewithal to digest what had happened, I was pulled into another round of surgery or treatment. For nearly two months, my mind attempted to catch up with the trauma that my body was enduring. Recovery was a painfully slow, deeply frustrating process. At about six weeks in, an occupational therapist arrived. She put a little Styrofoam peanut on a hospital tray and asked me to flick it. I stared at that simple little peanut and told my fingers to move, implored them to move, but nothing happened. I couldn't do it; I couldn't even come close. After she left, I was overwhelmed with discouragement and depression, fearing that I wasn't going to be able to function again. A few days later, it was time to try using my legs. I hadn't been able to stand since I had somehow lifted my body up on the tarmac. Several nurses and doctors gathered around me for my first attempt. The nurses pulled my legs over the bed. I took several deep breaths and looked up at the marshal on duty, standing guard at the door, smiling with encouragement. *You can do this,* I tried to convince myself. I placed my feet on the cold ground. *One foot in front of the other, Jackie.* With another deep breath of determination, I stood up . . . and immediately fainted.

My body just couldn't take it. A similar paralysis played out in my head whenever I tried to comprehend the massacre that had occurred in Guyana. I still don't feel that I ever properly mourned the devastating loss of Congressman Ryan, though I've honored him publicly, attended many tributes, and consciously worked to continue his legacy. I certainly didn't have the capacity to grasp his death while I was recovering at Arlington. My body, my mind, and my entire being felt like they were hanging on, moment to moment. Every thought was a struggle, and physically making it through each day was an all-consuming battle.

In mid-December, sweet, nurturing Aunt Tobie came and stayed with me for a week. She held on to my left hand tightly while my right was completely bandaged up and hanging from a sling above my hospital bed. She told me stories that have long since faded from memory, but they distracted me from my painful injuries and thoughts. It didn't matter what she said; her presence felt like a warm blanket was being placed over me, and served as an enticing reminder of the life at home that was waiting for me. Shortly after she left, Mom and Dad drove across the country to celebrate Christmas by my bedside, and they stayed in Virginia for almost two weeks. This time Mom was prepared and composed—plus she had my even-keeled, compassionate father to support her. Dad even cooked an amazing Christmas turkey and brought it to the hospital. It was among the most delicious meals I've ever eaten—because he had cooked it, but also because the very act of enjoying food and sitting with my parents signaled that I really was improving. When they left, though my terror at what I might encounter beyond the confines of the hospital was real, I knew that I'd soon be going home.

Literally two months after I had been shot, I was discharged from the hospital. I thanked all of the incredible doctors and nurses who had been my saviors and companions for the previous two months. I was in a wheelchair, still struggling to stand on my own for any extended amount of time. Given my blown radial nerve, I wore an apparatus on my arm that made it look like I was part Terminator beneath my skin. It was a sort of metal exoskeleton. Rubber bands held it together, and we had to regularly change them. There was a little sling for each finger. The contraption—I'm not sure what else to even call it—enabled me to lift things, which I otherwise would not have been able to do. Still in tremendous pain, I was at least mobile, and stable enough to start to piece together my life again.

I boarded a commercial flight home, accompanied by one of the US Marshals and Kathleen. As the plane descended into San Francisco, I had no idea what would be waiting for me. I will never forget the vision that unfolded before me as we entered the SFO terminal. It looked like some sort of demonstration, complete with mobs of waving signs and loud cheers. There were so many people, friends and strangers alike, waiting to greet me. The Sisters from Mercy had shown up. It appeared that every friend I had ever made was there, smiling or crying. I had never seen such a gathering of welcoming, kind faces. The love and frenzy of the whole scene was overwhelming, and I felt like my heart was going to burst with gratitude. The marshal wheeled me out, and I greeted as many people as I could, making my way through a haze of cameras and microphones that were shoved in my face, until we got to Katy's car and I could finally breathe. We drove to Katy's house, where I would be staying for a while. The death threats had continued, so the marshal had decided it would be too dangerous for me to stay with my parents.

Those first days back in the Bay Area were very hectic and consuming. Katy's home in South San Francisco was small, and all of us staying there was pushing its capacity. It was quite a crew, with Katy, the US Marshal, a man I had been dating casually, me, and a steady stream of family and friends who wanted to come by and help, all bumbling about Katy's two-bedroom home. All of the major media outlets reached out for interviews. I did a few, primarily over the phone. Afterward, I realized that when I had been engaged in conversation and answering questions, I hadn't really felt any physical pain. Of course it was still there, but I wasn't focused on it, so it didn't affect me as it had when I was lying in a hospital bed, with nothing to do but dwell on my discomfort and immobility. Especially with the media attention at such high volume, the daytime hours pulsed forward quickly. But the nights were long, and my mind refused to slow down. Lying in bed on Saturday, a few nights out of the hospital, reflecting on the interviews I had done and the uncertain landscape ahead, I thought through my options: *What should I do? What am I even able to do? This trauma isn't going away—so how can I turn it into something of value?*

As painful as my injuries were, and as much as I recoiled each time I got up and caught a glimpse of my shattered body, the only thing that felt debilitating was the terror that shadowed me at night. That relentless, incapacitating fear felt as much a part of me as the bullets that remained lodged in my body. Memories tortured me: the screams of anguish, the silence that followed, the bodies splayed around me. My nightmares were impossibly vivid, and I often awoke from them sweating, paralyzed with depression, and frightened that I wasn't ever going to be able to shake it.

As soon as the US Marshal, a lovely Southern woman, had helped situate me at Katy's, she left. I had been so lucky to have had her and the others—all equally kind and vigilant—as security blankets through the long hours of surgery and recuperation. By this time, the threats had ebbed away for the most part, as the details of the massacre had come to light. I still felt an extra edge of anxiety. Nobody, including the members, knew how things were going to unravel within the Temple. Police officers were a common presence when I was in public, and the risk of confrontation from the community held far more weight in the Bay Area. Though over nine hundred of the congregation had been murdered, there was still a large contingent of Peoples Temple members in the States, especially concentrated in San Francisco. The community members were beside themselves; this horrible tragedy had left them without a leader, without a church, seeking answers and someone to blame for the annihilation of their sisters and brothers. Still, even the angrier members of the Peoples Temple—the ones who insisted that they had been betrayed, or that there was a conspiracy at play, or that Congressman Ryan's delegation had destroyed their utopia and killed their loved ones—seemed disinclined to direct their rage my way. Not many were willing to carry forward more serious violence when faced with the incredible destruction in Guyana.

My recovery continued, though that very word is not an accurate description of the aftermath of being shot. I did not recover my old self; bullets rendered that impossible. That aside, I refused to spend the rest of my life as a victim of Guyana—there were too many of them. I had spent twenty-two hours staring at death, and many more on its threshold. I vowed to myself to use my resulting intimate awareness of life's fragility to take risks, to live each day with a fearless urgency. The other option was to shutter my windows and lock my doors, emotionally and otherwise. But Grandma's courage coursed through my veins. Besides, Dad hadn't sent me to judo only to have me cower from opposition. And Leo Ryan had refused to succumb to terror or to those who sought to wield it. I couldn't waste the blessing of being alive—now felt so acutely—by hiding away from the world, as desirable as that often, admittedly, seemed. That was not part of the plan. I had to take action, to do something, anything, so long as it got me to stand. I had to make every day worthwhile. I made that promise in Guyana, and I was going to keep it . . . I just needed to get out of bed first.

I arrived back in San Francisco on a Friday, and the following Monday was the last day to file papers to run for Ryan's congressional seat. It was a crowded race—with eleven candidates already vying for the seat—and my family felt it was too soon for such pressure. But I knew what Congressman Ryan would have done, and I had to move past the looming obstacles of fear and depression. As soon as I made the decision to run, my physical and emotional anxiety started retreating, just as my pain had in the interviews. I refused to be consumed by that anxiety. People talk about survivor guilt, or the self-hatred of the survivor. My belief that there is a larger plan at work—even if we're not privy to it—has saved me from those traps. It was not a mistake that my life had been spared. I didn't know why it had happened, but I was ready to spend the rest of my days living up to that fate. Choosing not to be stunted by my fear, not to spend any more of my time wallowing, I redirected my energy toward pulling together my first campaign run.

At ten on Monday morning, a few days after returning home, I went down to the county courthouse to sign the papers to run for Congress.

I couldn't even sign my own name yet—which is probably why plenty of people thought it might be premature for me to seek federal office. If Guyana hadn't happened, there is no way I would have *considered* running at that stage. I might still, as I write this, be a staffer or counsel in the House of Representatives; who knows? Before that trip, I had never felt certain about what I wanted to be. There was always a dream stirring inside, but it seemed so unattainable, such an enormous risk to put myself out there. I knew it was still a long shot, but I made up my mind to give it a try.

The special election race was an emotional, frenetic—and thankfully short—experience. The other eleven candidates had been campaigning since late November. I was the youngest candidate and the only woman running. Despite their concerns over my entering the race, my friends and family gave me exceptional support. They made up the bulk of my first campaign team, a run that was slapped together with bubble gum and baling wire. It was a ragtag group that included some of the Sisters from Mercy, an eighteen-year-old high school girl whom I had babysat when she was three years old, the Ryan children, and several people who wanted to help because of what I'd been through in Guyana. It was a real family affair, with no time to waste and delegated chores that ranged from precinct walks to doing the team's laundry.

We had six weeks to make a go at it, which meant making all of my printed material and devising a strategy very quickly, and I had comically limited funds. Our first feeble attempts at campaign literature were typed out on my red IBM Selectric typewriter. The pamphlets included a brief resume, as well as bullet points about some of the major issues for which I would fight: education, a decrease in government spending, housing, an end to job discrimination, and equal rights for women.

We distributed materials, spoke to constituents, and went door-to-door throughout the district. It required spending many late nights strategizing and banding together to perform all the tedious tasks of any campaign, which left me in a simultaneous state of animation and utter exhaustion. The whole campaign was a bit of a circus, with my arm in a sling and my legs often flaring up in pain. But that circus forced me to move on with my life.

We were up against a lot of unexpected hard-knock responses to my running. Despite serving as Ryan's legislative counsel in Congress, I was sidelined by critics who claimed I was just some unscrupulous assistant taking advantage of the tragic loss of my mentor for my own political gain. Others blew me off simply because I was young, and plenty disregarded or downplayed my capacity because I was a woman. I remember several other women telling me, with no small amount of vitriol, "I want you to know that I'm not going to vote for you just because you're a woman." Those needless digs usually left me speechless—there was no graceful way to respond. It was a tough way to learn that, very often, women are just as inclined as many men are to propagate political misogyny. On top of that, there were plenty of people who judged my run as ill advised because of the clearly debilitated state of my body. My arm was tough to hide, even under the many layers of clothing I used to obscure it. But none of those strikes against me gave me pause, especially once the campaign picked up energy.

Running for office forced me to look beyond myself, to campaign, socialize, make my opinions heard, and prove to myself—and everybody else—that I was not a victim. I felt duty bound to my promise to devote myself to public service, but I also genuinely hoped to carry forward Congressman Ryan's legacy. That same impulse was apparently shared by other members of his staff and family. A trifecta of Ryan-aligned candidates entered the race, each with their own hopes of stepping into our mentor's shoes. The race garnered national attention from the start: the American public was engrossed by Jones's tragic cult and its shocking end, so the runoff among Congressman Ryan's staffers made for a good story. Much of the race came down to some pretty adolescent perceptions about who had been closest to him. Ryan's kids threw their support behind me, while Ryan's mother and his ex-wife endorsed

My mom, Nancy, and dad, Fred, when they were dating, in the Inner Sunset flats my mom owned.

My dad in San Francisco shortly after immigrating to the United States.

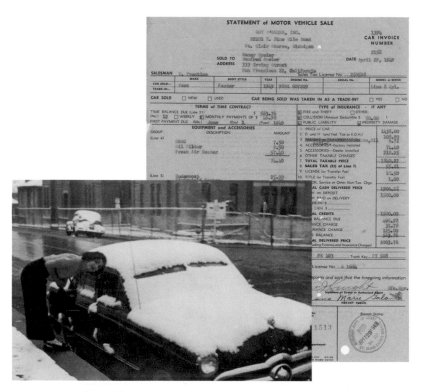

My mom making her way back to San Francisco from her honeymoon and experiencing her first snow with my parents' Ford, their first and only new car, in 1949.

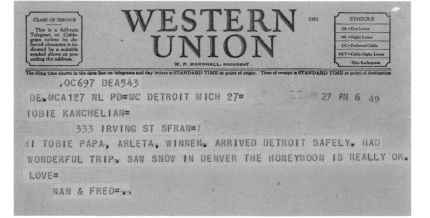

Mom and me, in the Inner Sunset flat shortly after I was born, showing off her two new possessions: me and a brand-new TV set.

My dear aunt Tobie, a perfect model of grace, warmth, and wit.

In 1951 with Santa. I have always, clearly, preferred Halloween.

Grandma Speier, who helped shape my resilience, faith, and love of politics, watching as I was sworn in to the board of supervisors in 1980.

Grandma Speier and me after my first Holy Communion in 1958. A proud moment with my spiritual lodestar.

Mrs. Kennedy is deeply appreciative of
your sympathy and grateful
for your thoughtfulness

The note Jackie Kennedy's office sent me after I'd written to give my condolences on her husband's death, and the franked signature that I practiced copying for hours in my bedroom.

My first foray into politics, on the campaign trail with Leo Ryan and the other Ryan Girls, 1966.

Next to my great friend Kathleen Wentworth when we were cheerleaders at our all-girls high school, Mercy, 1967 (far left).

Dancing with Dad. One of the highlights each year was the Mercy father-daughter dance.

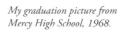

My graduation picture from Mercy High School, 1968.

With Leo Ryan in 1973, this time as one of his staffers in Washington, DC, before I moved back to San Francisco to attend law school.

Talking strategy on the plane to Guyana to investigate Jim Jones and the Peoples Temple, with Leo Ryan.

Members of the Peoples Temple in Jonestown, preparing for a community meal.

The laughter of children rings through the air from the playground, where tunnels and lattices, swings and balance beams provide creative and healthy recreation. In the schoolhouse, a full curriculum of study is guaranteed to every young person, both elementary and high school age. Indeed, learning is ongoing at Jonestown, and evening classes which offer languages, crafts, and other skills are filled with students of all ages, including senior citizens.

"Our children are our greatest treasure", proclaims a poster on the nursery wall. The limitless potential of youth is celebrated daily and expressed in the devotion of all the adults to the welfare, health, and security of the children.

Tom Grubbs (*left*), a specialist who taught physically handicapped children in the U.S., designed the playground equipment. It is not only fun to play on, but builds motor skills and coordination needed by all children. Tom is one of over a dozen teachers with advanced degrees. Many of the youngsters who were simply not motivated to learn before coming here, have delved into subjects of interest to them, and are becoming excellent and attentive students in the Jonestown School. Education for residents of all ages is a high priority.

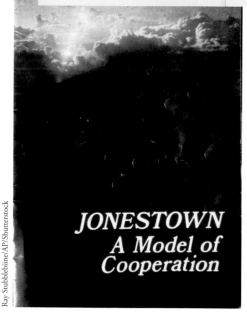

JONESTOWN
A Model of Cooperation

Examples of the propaganda pamphlets that we were given before flying to Port Kaituma. Each picture told the story of idyllic communal living that was hard to reconcile with the hours of depositions I'd taken from defectors and family members in San Francisco.

The sign that greeted us at the entry to Jonestown as we peered out the back of the truck.

Leo Ryan addressing the members of Jonestown in front of the sign reading "Those Who Do Not Remember the Past are Condemned to Repeat It" moments before the first defector approached journalist Don Harris.

MEMORANDUM

Mom + Dad —

I love you. Should anything happen be proud because my life has been full of the love you have given me. I have no regrets.

Love, Jackie.

$1,000 life ins policy w/ credit union. Fireside certificates in 2nd desk drawer.

The eerily prophetic note I left my parents in my Capitol Hill desk drawer before embarking on the congressional delegation to Guyana.

The plane that I sought refuge under during the shooting.

Helping load one of the planes with defectors from Jonestown (I'm in the background), moments before the shooting began.

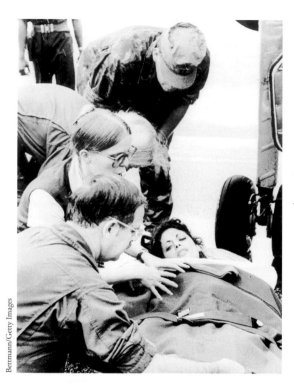

After over twenty hours without medical attention, I was finally airlifted out of Guyana by the United States military medevac team.

TEMPLE-SPEIER

(SAN FRANCISCO)-- AC AIDE TO SLAIN CONGRESSMAN LEO RYAN WITNESSED HIS MURDER NEAR THE PEOPLES TEMPLE SETTLEMENT IN GUYANA AND WAS HERSELF SERIOUSLY WOUNDED. BUT IT'S REPORTED TODAY THAT EVEN THOUGH HER LIFE WAS THREATENED, SHE WAS LEFT UNGUARDED AT A WASHINGTON-AREA HOSPITAL.

THE SAN FRANCISCO CHRONICLE SAYS U-S MARSHALS WERE DISPATCHED TO GUARD JACKIE SPEIER ONLY AFTER RYAN'S FAMILY COMPLAINED TO THE WHITE HOUSE THAT HER LIFE WAS IN DANGER AND THAT SHE WAS UNPROTECTED. MS. SPEIER WAS RYAN'S LEGISLATIVE COUNSEL.

THE CONGRESSMAN'S ADMINISTRATIVE ASSISTANT, JOE HOLSINGER, SAID IT TOOK MORE THAN 24 HOURS OF WRANGLING WITH WHITE HOUSE AND JUSTICE DEPARTMENT OFFICIALS TO POST FEDERAL GUARDS OUTSIDE MS. SPEIER'S HOSPITAL ROOM.

UPI 12-06 04:38 APS

Testifying in front of Congress at the "Information Meeting on Cult Phenomenon in the United States," 1979.

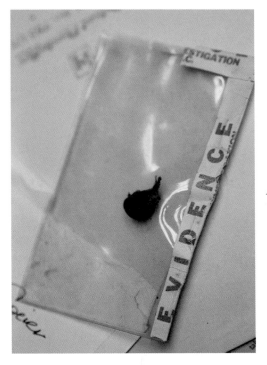

One of the dumdum bullets that was retrieved from my body—a stark reminder that it takes only a small piece of metal to cause an immeasurable amount of pain, damage, and loss.

Still recovering from my injuries and days after returning home to San Francisco, I signed papers to declare my candidacy in the race to fill Leo Ryan's seat in Congress—an election I lost.

UPI/Jack Holper/Getty Images

Joe Holsinger—Ryan's former fifty-seven-year-old chief of staff, who relentlessly brought Ryan's name into his campaign. Ryan's attorney, a gregarious former mayor named George Corey, was also running. The three of us each emphasized our allegiance to the fallen congressman, which placed a heightened pressure on the race and its outcome.

Holsinger took an incredibly aggressive, offensive stance and claimed that Corey and I misrepresented our connections to the congressman. He insinuated that Corey was a puppet for high political interests and the Arab American lobby. It was ludicrous. His brochure described me as young, clever, and ambitious—as if those were shameful qualities—and suggested I was trying to convert sympathy for my Guyana wounds into support for an office for which I lacked experience. His baseless, ethnically charged, and sexist smears, coupled with his relentless attempts to align himself with Congressman Ryan, backfired and repelled more voters than they attracted. While we Democrats were the subjects of a lot of questionable, off-topic press, San Mateo County Supervisor Bill Royer, also fifty-seven, was the Republican favorite. His fundraising abilities alone put him in prime position to take the seat.

I rallied for the six remaining weeks, running with the slogan, "Keep Courage in Congress." The idea of debates had terrified me, but I'd worked in Washington and learned by osmosis from my years in Ryan's office. Participating in the candidates' forums, I found myself just as capable and up to speed as all of the other candidates, if not more so. I was much more prepared than I'd expected. I knew the issues intimately, having spent years addressing constituents' concerns. I could confidently respond to questions about environmental interests, tax reform, or the foreign assistance budget. It was a very affirming experience, one which solidified my belief that I had something to offer in the political realm. I could see that there was value in putting myself out there and speaking openly, even when self-doubt was pulling me back, even when my first instincts told me to stay hidden. Stepping into the fray when I felt least prepared to do so proved to be a powerful watershed. My standing was respectable. I came in third for the Democrats. Republican Bill Royer ultimately won, capturing 57 percent of the vote and filling Congressman Ryan's seat for the duration of the term. Despite losing in the primary, the process had confirmed what I needed to be doing with my life. I was committed. Furthermore, that would not be the last time the district saw my name on the ballot.

Mom and Dad, who were never much of an emotional support system, really came through for me after the election. They were always there for me when I needed them, without fail or fanfare. They had quietly put a down payment on a condo in Burlingame and gave me the keys—a space of my own when I was ready for it. I took over the payments once I moved in, but having that home was an essential piece to the puzzle of feeling like I could begin an independent life. After nearly six weeks of living in Katy's house and going through the buzz of a whole election campaign, I was ready to settle into my own place. I'd gotten stronger and didn't need the wheelchair any longer. Despite an air of fear about being alone, and with no certainty around my professional future, I moved into my new home and my new existence.

Unfortunately, I was still restricted by the physical trauma, and I was under a doctor's care, which meant prioritizing regular hospital visits. Because of my injuries, I had to change little details about my lifestyle, things I had never thought about all that much. My legs were highly sensitive to touch, which meant that, for the longest time, I could not wear jeans, let alone tights or nylons. I could not fully extend my arm, an adjustment that kept me in physical therapy for years. Even now, forty years later, residual issues remain: I still can't fully extend two of my fingers, but it's a microscopic concern in the grand scheme of things. I had worked hard to fight my way back, so by the time I had my own place, I was able to accomplish necessary daily functions without asking for help.

Dealing with the repercussions of emotional trauma proved far more challenging. I still never know when that deep sense of fright might hit me, and that feeling was especially profound for the first year or two of recovery. I often felt close to the edge of a panic attack, and without the distraction of running for office, it was harder to predict or manage my moods. And once you've been shot, your body never forgets. I remember lying beside the little pool at my condo on the Fourth of July, about eight months following the massacre. Nobody else was around, but someone relatively nearby set off a bunch of fireworks. I felt like I had just been electrocuted. I jolted up. My body trembled and twitched, and without warning I started to cry as the fireworks continued popping. I couldn't rid myself of the visceral memory. Eventually my heartbeat slowed to normal, and I pulled myself together enough to go inside. Perpetually being on the edge of a flashback was exhausting. The only thing that genuinely seemed to help was focusing my energy elsewhere, which for me meant immersing myself in work, in politics. I suppose I did inherit some of my parents' work ethic.

I stopped by Mom and Dad's for visits whenever I could, but those trips soon brought their own measure of stress. Shortly after my return, Mom called me in hysterics to tell me that my dad had been dating another woman. When my mother discovered the affair, she immediately sent my dad packing. He moved into Grandma's house in San Francisco. Mom was understandably distraught, so I started going to see her more often. My arm was still in a sling, and I was coping with my own emotional and physical issues. Even in that state, however, she didn't like to see me idle. One afternoon she was in a frenzy and, as I tried to calm her down, she insisted that I needed to vacuum the house. Mom loved me, but was so used to relating to me in a certain way— helping me achieve, demanding I try my best, raising the bar—that she couldn't navigate a dynamic where life dictated that we both had new, different needs. Finally, it was my old-school German grandma who told Dad, in no uncertain terms, "You go back. *Go back!*" So Dad went back and asked for my mom's forgiveness, and my parents reconciled, at least enough to keep them going. It was a small relief, but I couldn't get too wrapped up in that quagmire. It was time to return to putting my own life back together.

In 1979, I decided to run for a seat on the San Mateo County Board of Supervisors. I would be challenging Jim Fitzgerald, the twenty-year incumbent. Nobody, not even me at times, really thought I had a shot. But I had a much more organized campaign that time around, supported by most of the same amazing, hardworking group of about a dozen volunteers who have been with me since my first election and have stuck with me through each campaign of my political career. I also had the benefit of a number of people from the environmental community who urged me to run to unseat Fitzgerald, who had done nothing for their causes. A few new faces joined the team. When we were stuffing envelopes one night, a young man walked in wearing a suit, spoke with familiarity about campaigns, and had with him a check for a hundred dollars. The professional attire and *enormous* sum of money were so out of step with our grassroots atmosphere that we entertained the idea that he had been sent over by one of the other candidates to snoop around. His name is Brian Perkins, and he's been a devoted part of the core crew for my every election since then, and currently serves as my district director. We still jokingly refer to him as The Spy.

That year, we started calling the team ACSS, short for Aides to County Supervisor Speier. We were all of the same generation, with some of our parents involved as well. It became a family of sorts—we would get together throughout the year and have potlucks, even when it wasn't an election season. In later years we would take annual vacations to Mexico. For that first campaign, we were young and had little idea what we were doing, but ACSS was brimming with energy and commitment. Politics absolutely requires a village. It's so necessary to get a diverse range of opinions on a given issue. And at the end of the day, it's a lot more fun. I don't work alone—I never have, and I never will. Youthful energy can bring a tremendous amount to the legislative arena. We weren't quite organized yet, but we were on our way.

The race for supervisor was notably more sophisticated than our first try—I even hired a campaign manager from Sacramento, David Townsend. Instead of leaning *entirely* on the support of nuns and cheerleading alums who all had day jobs, we had a professional guiding us. We had an official campaign headquarters, in a dingy upstairs room that was above a barbeque restaurant and was likely a massage parlor before we set up shop. It was one big room into which we hauled a bunch of donated folding tables and chairs. Personally and physically, I was in much better shape for the race and felt prepared for most of the requisite aspects of campaigning. But I was still a miserable fundraiser. Had I been given a box of cacti, I'd have gone around the block and returned with twenty bucks and an empty box; but when it came to selling myself, I still hadn't found my footing. I met a man at an event who promised to contribute five hundred dollars to my campaign. When I called him to follow up, at the end of hearing my spiel, he sighed and said he'd be willing to give me a hundred bucks. Which is all to underscore that there's no way I could have pulled off an adequately funded campaign if not for ACSS—those dedicated volunteers who had so little to gain and were truly loyal, committed friends with the ability to turn their belief in me into contributions and eventual votes. We spent endless hours mailing, labeling, making phone calls, and taking countless walks through each precinct in the city to promote my candidacy.

We had our work cut out for us. The local paper, the *San Mateo Times*, was business oriented, and my opponent, Jim Fitzgerald, had been a real estate and insurance man before running for office. The paper was so fully behind him that, throughout the campaign, their headlines referred to me only as "Fitzgerald's opponent" instead of putting my name in print. Initially, Fitzgerald was equally dismissive. A woman and political neophyte, in his eyes, wasn't going to beat a household name who had served for twenty years and was backed by the deep pockets of county developers. But I never gave up, and neither did my team. We rallied support, canvassing the district using the training Mom had instilled in me through my door-to-door sales background. My team and I spent months talking and listening to the constituents. Days before the election, we managed to put out a sensational double-truck ad in that same local paper. There had been an error in one of my brochure printings, so we had a credit that allowed us to finance that big splash of an ad. Fitzgerald had a terrible attendance record at the regional meetings the board of supervisors were required to serve on, so we hit him on his poor record and implied that he had a lack of concern about the issues, in addition to pushing my agenda. Instead of staying gathered at that dump of a headquarters on the day of the primary, we went to a landmark restaurant called Bertolucci's. A huge group of us was there, waiting on the results via phone call from somebody down at the election office in Redwood City. Late in the evening, we finally got word that I had eked out a win in the primary. I couldn't believe it; the whole team was just ecstatic.

The election in November was far less of a nail biter. We did more of the same grassroots-style campaigning, but I was running just against Fitzgerald and had established my politics and myself. The race was never close; I won by over twenty-one thousand votes. It had been two years since Guyana. I was thirty years old, the youngest person ever elected to the county's board of supervisors.

I've had a paperweight on my desk for decades that reads, *What would you attempt to do if you knew you could not fail?* If I had not lost that race for Congress, I never would have been prepared to run for county supervisor. I felt like I had been chosen to deliver a new energy and perspective to what was essentially a board of older men. In the race for Ryan's seat, I was fueled by wild determination and a desperate need for distraction. But from the moment I was sworn in as a supervisor, I finally felt like I could move forward in my life with confidence and build my own legislative record.

Chapter Six

LOVE AND POLITICS

As prepared as I was to take my position on the board, returning to the public eye felt strange. I had been watched, then scrutinized, during the relentless coverage of Jonestown and its aftermath, but I was still adjusting to how my injured arm and legs looked, which didn't help matters. I had never had a great relationship with, or regard for, my body. After returning from Guyana, my tenuous emotional state meant that I avoided even looking in the mirror.

My dating life suffered, though there was notably heightened interest in me after I got back from Guyana. It was difficult to entertain a serious relationship, or even a promising one, when I felt like damaged goods. I was afraid to be intimate with anyone, always anxious about how my body would be perceived. During those early years of healing, I dated a few men with whom I felt some connection, but my preoccupation with my injuries was a real barrier. If ever it seemed like I was going to progress past a few casual dates with a guy, I would have to explain that, before we got physical, there was something he should see. There was a stark difference between hearing about my wounds and actually viewing them, especially during the first few years following Jonestown. I was compulsively alert to how men touched my scars. If it turned a man's stomach—if there was reluctance, or if he recoiled—then I knew it wasn't going to work out. I needed to know whether any suitor accepted them, and accepted me as I was. This wasn't a question of vanity. Coming to grips with the tangible reminders of my trauma was a big deal for me, and showing another person evidence of the tragedy made me feel vulnerable. Revealing my scars unsettled me.

As difficult as that was, I persisted. Dating was important to me and gave me another impetus to force myself out into public. Though a few men piqued my interest along the way, it wasn't until I ran for supervisor that I first experienced real love. One of the members on the board who, notably, did not endorse me during my campaign was Supervisor Ed Bacciocco. Ed was a real up-and-coming star in the Democratic Party. He was a professor, he had written a book, he was attractive, he was erudite, and he was impossibly charming—the whole package. When I had approached him for his endorsement, he told me that he couldn't support me. He didn't think I could win because—in his perception—I wouldn't be "hardworking enough." I was insulted by the snub and his ignorant assumptions, but at least he was straightforward about his reason. So it was a bit of a rocky start for Ed and me as colleagues. It didn't take long for him to adjust his opinion. Once I was elected, he and I jointly took on an issue: how best to deal with a controversial development on my district's San Bruno Mountain, an undeveloped area on the San Francisco Peninsula, with rolling hills and an endangered-species issue. Working together, fighting for the same cause, we were immediately attracted to each other, both intellectually and physically, and our relationship quickly advanced beyond the professional realm.

This was different than anything I had experienced. We fell deeply in love—the kind of love that sustains infatuation and then surpasses it. We thought it would be best to keep our love a secret, worried that making it public might complicate matters on the board. If it didn't work out, introducing more colleagues to our romance could set up an uncomfortable situation. When we got together, we would meet at one of our homes or go into the city, where we wouldn't be spotted or recognized. It was a fanciful romance: he wrote me beautiful love poems and sent me flowers every week, without fail. I was besotted with him, and with being in love. Though Guyana had molded me in untold ways, my experience there retreated from the forefront of my mind as Ed and my political endeavors gradually took precedence.

It was a short and intense courtship, and within months Ed proposed. It felt so right—crazy and wonderful and restorative. Finally, my life was coming together, in the sweetest way possible. We decided that rather than share our news among a few people and allow it to trickle out into the public, Ed would call a press conference in the chamber of the board of supervisors. Though I had publicly stated the day before that I had a personal announcement to make, nobody—not our colleagues, the press, or even our families—had any idea that Ed and I were seeing each other. But it was clear that we were in love when we walked out together, both of us laughing and beaming, with Ed grasping my left hand. The local media was there as he stepped forward and announced our engagement. It shocked everybody, on the board and beyond. The next morning, on the front page of the *San Mateo Times*, was a photograph of the two of us giggling, with a headline that read, "County Supervisors Speier, Bacciocco Tell Marriage Plans."

It was a relatively explosive story within the county: two supervisors, living in different districts, planned to marry. There were plenty of questions, and a bit of griping in the press about how we were going to maintain our residences and whether the integrity of our political lives and districts would be compromised. But I think our love story also captivated the community, and Ed was always ready with a quip to distract from any aggressive questions about where we would be living or how we would conduct our careers.

Unfortunately, Ed had been diagnosed with lupus and Crohn's disease later in life and was experiencing some debilitating effects. He had

a lot of physical issues, so he decided that it would be in his best interest
to take a break from the strains of political life and opted out of the race
for reelection. That decision smoothed over any potential complications
for us professionally. But it was very difficult for him. He owned horses
and loved riding, and had maintained an active life overall, so it was
definitely an adjustment for him. At one point he tried to persuade me
to end our relationship, claiming that he didn't want me to have to care
for a sick man. The very notion was absurd to me—I was totally devoted
and had no second thoughts about our marriage.

Ed's favorite place in the world was Hawaii, and we went there a
number of times over the course of our courtship and engagement.
In the fall of 1982, I was walking down the beach by myself on the
Big Island. We had been together for nearly two years. The lavender-
streaked sky signaled a nearing sunset, but the beach and ocean were
still crowded with people enjoying themselves. My arms and my legs
were covered by a bright sarong with large flowers on it that reached
past my knees. The beauty of that moment transfixed me, and I mar-
veled over the simple gift of being there, being alive, and being in love.
But I was still preoccupied with everything I was hiding. It had taken
me several years to come to terms with the damage those five bullets
had done to my body. But as I took in the beauty that surrounded me,
a simple joy overcame me, and I ignored the voice that was always telling me that I would be prevented from living a full life—breaking the
yoke of depression that had set in when I was back at Arlington. My
practical voice, assisted by the beauty surrounding me, cut through the
remaining static of my insecurities. *You can't let yourself be hampered by
this forever. You cannot live your life as some disfigured, frightened victim
who has to hide. You have to embrace that this is exactly who you are.*

I slowly untied my sarong, which felt as heavy as a suit of armor,
and dropped it in the wet sand behind me. I continued down the beach
in my bathing suit, noticing a few people who did a double take, staring
at the remnant scars on my legs and arm. I kept going, also noticing

that there were plenty of people who didn't stare at all. I squeezed the sand between my toes and felt the water rushing up to meet me. I started running down the beach feeling free, perhaps freer than I ever had. What a miracle that I could even walk. What a miracle that I was alive and on this beautiful beach, with a meaningful career and a man to whom I felt entirely devoted. Those bullets, those strips of pink skin, those cobbled scars—they were a part of me. I remembered my vow that if I survived, I would not waste another minute. Concealing myself and everything I'd endured was a waste of time. I had to put all of that behind me. I had too much living to do.

Our marriage would be Ed's third. My faith had remained a center of gravity for me, and, while I wasn't deterred by Ed's previous divorces, I felt some conviction that my marriage needed to be sanctioned by the church. So Ed began the process of annulling his previous marriages—a necessity in the Catholic Church for anyone with a previous marriage. That process took longer than we would have liked, relative to our eagerness to get married. As we waited for all the paperwork to come through, we started looking at homes together. As the months ticked by, I found the perfect embroidered Priscilla of Boston wedding dress, and we anxiously waited for our day to arrive.

About a year and a half after our public announcement, we were at my condo in South San Francisco. I was on my way to the city for a presentation and asked Ed to join me. He couldn't, because he had plans to go to dinner with his father. We agreed to meet back up later that night, and I left for the event. Once I arrived, I got up to deliver my presentation, and—much to my shock—I saw Ed's father sitting at one of the round tables in the audience. The sight of him knocked the wind out of me, and I felt a strange blend of numbness and nausea. I couldn't understand what was going on. *Did I misunderstand Ed?*

After my presentation I managed to exchange some polite words with Ed's father, but I was operating completely on autopilot. As soon as I could leave, I drove myself back to my condo. An hour or two later, Ed arrived. He walked in the door and flashed me one of his characteristic grins.

"How was dinner with your dad?" I asked him, unable to attempt small talk.

"Oh, really nice," he said.

"Huh. That's funny," I said quietly. "Because your dad was at my event."

Ed sat down and put his head in his hands. He broke immediately and became incredibly emotional. I barely said a word as he confessed that he had been with another woman. I had no idea how to respond; I could feel myself unraveling, my brain reeling with questions. *This cannot be happening. I'm engaged to marry this man, to spend my life with him, and he's off with another woman? How? How did I not know? How could he treat me like this? And how could I have been so naive?* Bowled over with disbelief, I didn't yell or tell him to get the hell outta there. Not yet. He stayed on the couch at the condo that night while I went to bed and wept, only letting up for moments, mad at myself for being weak, before the sobbing recommenced. It had all been such a dream, the one that I had imagined for so long about falling madly in love and sharing my life with someone. That dream, one that I'd drawn such confidence and courage from, was ripped away from me. My relationship with Ed had helped me see myself—not as damaged goods, but as a smart, desirable, powerful woman—and now that confidence felt threatened. *Has it all been a lie?* It was a harsh awakening from love, and not one I felt equipped to handle.

Ed and I were done. I couldn't ignore the fact that he had fallen out of love with me. After that night of sobbing, doubting myself and everything that had happened over the last year, I regained my wits. I knew that my strength—my worth and path in life—wasn't tied to Ed's love and approval; it was tied to my service to others, to my career. I gave Ed back the ring almost immediately, feeling exhausted, emotionally and physically. He didn't help matters, or leave me alone to process and move on with my life. We had to work together for several more months, which was tough, especially since he also continued sending me flowers once a week, which was brutal. He was sensitive in some ways, but his gestures only held me back. I was thrown into despondency at the sight of each new bouquet.

Then there was the awkward sting of the public aftermath, as everybody found out that we had called our long engagement off. That's the kicker of revealing a relationship at a press conference: your romantic relationship—especially when both parties are public figures—lands on the doorstep of everybody who reads the local news. The media threw swarms of judgments at me, and plenty of assumptions were made as the county analyzed my heartbreak. One columnist speculated that I had ended our relationship because Ed was in poor health. None of those reports were accurate, but neither of us were inclined to comment at the time—it wouldn't have been appropriate or helped keep our relationship out of the press. Gossip burns fast and bright, but it goes out just as quickly. I later found out that he had been seeing the woman who cared for his horses. My personal anguish and humiliation stayed with me for a while. It was a painful time—I had felt so certain that what we had was perfect. I was wrong.

To distract myself from the torment at home, I threw myself into my legislative work. Maneuvering around powerful Bay Area political dealers gave me back a little of my confidence, despite their petty misogyny, which went as far as them coining a new nickname for me, Poodle, derived from my thick, distinct eighties hair. It didn't take me long to find my political footing and turn my focus toward my constituents' needs.

One of the first issues I took on was a local utility company whose transformer had leaked PCBs—a coolant fluid—into a constituent's backyard. When questioned, the company denied that the substance was harmful, but when they finally sent a crew to clean it up, the workers arrived in hazmat suits. When I heard the homeowner's description of watching the cleanup crew, afraid to even breathe in the substance, and the way the family had been casually exposed to such toxins, I was enraged. How could a company, in good conscience, assure these people that there was no risk involved? It seemed, at the very least, grossly negligent and deceitful.

After initial talks with the constituent and representatives from the energy company, alongside some research into PCBs, I introduced an ordinance that required the company to identify every transformer with PCBs in the county and replace the hazardous liquid with a nontoxic alternative. The company responsible for such reckless polluting turned out to be Pacific Gas and Electric—a genuine Goliath I would face off with many times over the course of my career. During that time, I realized that there are few greater thrills than confronting seemingly immovable opponents and succeeding in changing their behavior. To do so requires a relentless disposition, a backbone, and a willingness to fail.

That early confrontation offered me two other essential lessons that I still call upon: first, to trust my intuition, which includes allowing my gut—or what I call my "outrage meter"—to be my guide; and second, to not be intimidated by confrontation with authority or very powerful interests. I've come to even enjoy it. Working with Congressman Ryan and surviving Guyana equipped me with a kind of fearlessness when it comes to challenging adversaries—a quality that I had only just begun to rely on, but that has been crucial throughout my career.

I was coming into my own as a legislator, taking on the day-to-day concerns of my constituents and sinking my teeth into the bigger issues plaguing the state at large, but in my personal life, I sat on the sidelines for a while. Roughly a year following my breakup with Ed, I became involved with a man named Steve, through tremendously unromantic circumstances. I was one of two female members of the board and vocal about women's rights. A deputy district attorney came to my office one afternoon to talk about the difficulties the district attorney's office was having in getting rape convictions in our county. He thought the issue stemmed from an inadequate chain of custody when recovering and logging evidence. The problem, he believed, was occurring when women were taken to the hospital after reporting a rape. That seemed solvable to me, so I scheduled a meeting with one of our county hospitals' administrators and staff to see how we could fix the issue and ensure more convictions.

Among the committee members was Dr. Steve Sierra, the chief of staff and head of the Emergency Department at Chope County Hospital, where most rape examinations took place. We met a few times so he could walk me through the procedure, and at one of those meetings he mentioned that a Southern California county, Ventura, had a superior system of collecting evidence and, consequently, significantly higher conviction rates. In addition to a proper chain of custody for the evidence, Chope Hospital needed to properly train its staff in documenting evidence of a forcible rape during exams. Steve had seen a video that one of the Ventura doctors had created about best practices for the whole process, detailing how to perform the exam with respect and efficiency. The video sounded like a valuable tool, something that could help us align our system with theirs. So, Steve called my office a couple of weeks later once he had a copy.

"Great, I'll find a time to come down to the hospital and view it."

"I don't know, it's pretty hectic here—you'd probably be interrupted if you came to the hospital," he said.

"Well, I don't have a VCR at home."

"That's no problem—I can bring one over."

"Okay . . ." I said slowly. It seemed strange, but we had been having all of these meetings, and I was eager to come up with a viable solution to present to the full board of supervisors, so I gave Steve my address. That night, he showed up at my townhouse with the training videotape, a VCR, and two bottles of Château Haut-Brion. Steve was never one for subtlety. We watched the video, taking notes while drinking this incredible wine, and—despite the background and the surreal peculiarity of the whole evening—I have to admit that I was pretty captivated by this guy. At the end of the night, he packed up his VCR and suggested that we get together again soon.

For our first real date, he took me to a sushi restaurant. I had never eaten sushi before, but I figured he was testing how adventurous my tastes were, and I'm not one to back down from a challenge. At one point, he offered me some foamy-looking sea urchin with a quail's egg on top. It couldn't have looked more unappealing. *I really like this guy*, I thought. *He seems like a risk-taker.* Having grown up with Dad's weekly dose of fried liver, you'd think I wouldn't flinch at a piece of sea urchin, but it was the grossest thing I had ever tasted. Despite my sour, displeased face, Steve smiled at me, and I felt like I had passed the test. That was the first night I really forgot about Ed and let myself go. Steve's energy was electric, contagious, and seductive. At the same time, he was as easy to talk to as my oldest friend. I was smitten—or certainly on my way there.

Unfortunate circumstances made it possible for me to see Steve again. A few weeks after our sushi date, I got a call from my dad. My grandmother was living with my parents at the time. Decades before, my grandfather had suffered a stroke. Every day that he was in the hospital, Grandma had taken two buses from their home on Thirty-Ninth and Noriega to go visit him. There's a very steep climb to get from the bus stop to the Laguna Honda Hospital. But she walked it without fail, all one hundred eighty pounds of her, devoted and powerful enough to climb up the steepest hills to go and sit beside her husband during visiting hours. After he died, she lived on her own until her early nineties, when my dad moved her into their house in Belmont. Dad created a little suite for her downstairs, where she had a bedroom, a living room, and a bathroom. Without fail, she'd sit there and listen to her gospel of KGO news radio. She drank a pot of coffee throughout the day, listening to the news of the world. Every day my father would make her breakfast, lunch, and dinner and bring it all down to her. She had been living with my parents for a few years when, on the day after Christmas, she woke up with her stomach distended. Something clearly wasn't right. She didn't eat breakfast and was in a lot of pain. I was frightened and knew Steve was on duty that day, so I insisted we take her to Chope immediately. I hadn't seen Steve since our sushi date, but I needed someone I could trust, who would look after Grandma properly. When we arrived, Steve was clearly surprised to see me. He examined Grandma and diagnosed her with a gallbladder issue, despite some disagreement from the surgeon on staff. After further testing, Grandma had to have her gallbladder removed and was treated in the hospital for a couple of days. I stayed with her the whole time, and Steve checked in on her, making sure her recovery was progressing. That episode, and Steve's level-headed response, drew me closer to him.

We continued dating throughout 1984. I was intrigued by him, and we had a blast together, but he had made it clear that he wasn't looking for anything serious. Still, I invited him to come with me when President Ronald Reagan awarded Leo Ryan a posthumous Congressional Gold Medal. It was a dramatic and emotional event for me, and Steve knew there would be some heavy moments. But he was excited to be my escort, and we had the time of our lives. We flew into and stayed in New York, then took the commuter flight down to DC. We drank champagne in the taxi on the way to the White House ceremony. There's a photo of the two of us smiling away with a large group: the whole Ryan family, several congressmen, and President Reagan. That night, I took him around DC to show him the historic sites—the Lincoln Memorial, Washington Monument, and Jefferson Memorial, all dramatically lit—then we flew back to New York to catch a Broadway show. It was a ridiculous whirlwind, and I was falling for him—hard.

Steve, I was learning, lived on the edge, or at least dangerously close to it. He was athletic, a marathon runner who ran races around the world, whereas I was very hesitant when it came to sports, especially with my injuries. He encouraged me to train for the Bay to Breakers, San Francisco's annual seven-and-a-half-mile run. It was a wild race where many of the participants showed up in costume; it was essentially a street party in motion, in celebration of the city's vibrant residents. I trained, with Steve's help and encouragement, and showed up for the fun. I ran with Steve's voice in my mind, pushing me forward. I was nowhere near the front of the pack, but I crossed that finish line. I wanted to prove, to both of us, that I could be athletic. Then I went home and passed out on the couch for hours.

Though I knew Steve wasn't looking for a serious relationship, our lives became increasingly entwined. That year, Steve took me with him on his annual pilgrimage to Wimbledon. He had an exhausting obsession with the tournament. I was thrilled. As if Wimbledon wasn't enough of a fairy tale, after the finals we took the Venice Simplon-Orient-Express from London to Paris, where we walked the streets and dined out every night. It was just . . . storybook stuff. I was completely bonkers for him, truly swept off my feet. I had never been treated like that before.

By 1985, our relationship had evolved into an exclusive one. I even, absurdly, learned how to make sushi and made him a fabulous platter (skipping the sea urchin). It took me hours, and I drove it over to the county hospital, just to delight him. I wanted to keep our relationship fresh, but at the same time, I was holding down a demanding job as a county supervisor.

That same summer, Steve and I were scheduled to take a vacation in Hawaii. A few days before we left, he called to check in, as he often did between patients at the hospital. After less than a minute, I sensed something odd in his voice—a lack of his typical zeal, a hesitancy to respond.

"Steve, what is going on?" I asked him.

"Jackie, I . . . I'd like to take a rain check on Hawaii."

I immediately understood; we had gotten too serious and he wanted a break. The fairy tale was over. That was clear in his voice, and in the very notion of his taking a "rain check" on our holiday. As far as I was concerned, we were done. I wasn't interested in waiting for him to flit around until he was ready. Since we had already booked our flights, and they weren't cheap, I went to Hawaii alone. I felt so devastated by the rejection, and so shocked by that call, that I didn't know what else to do with myself; I spent a week crying into piña coladas. There was something much more crushing about being heartbroken in paradise, watching couples hold hands on the beach at sunset. I was a pathetic mess, and I needed to come to grips with the end of our relationship by myself. When I returned, I still felt like a vessel that had been carved out. I behaved like an adolescent, doing things like driving by the hospital on my way home just to see if his car was there. I knew I was lucky to have felt so deeply for another person, and I was not especially proud of my antics.

Again, I channeled all of my energy and focus into my work life, putting in late nights at the office and attending every meeting possible. Three months passed like that, and in late October, I was chosen to go to a Women's Campaign Fund conference at Harvard. WCF is a national nonpartisan organization dedicated to increasing the number of women in elected office. The training at the conference involved finding ways to reach common-ground solutions and support other women at all levels of government. The trip was encouraging, fascinating, and exhausting in equal measure, and once I had made my way back across the country, I got home and took a long nap. At about five or six in the evening, just as it was starting to get dark, the phone rang. I leaned across my bed, half asleep. It was Steve. I pulled myself up and he started chatting, as though we hadn't missed a beat. He asked if we could get together the following weekend. I already had plans—I was going to the Big Game (Cal vs. Stanford). In my groggy state, I told him he could come along if he wanted. He did.

That Saturday, we met at the game and went to a lively tailgate party, where everybody was drinking and enjoying themselves in the fall sunshine. I had been nervous about seeing him, confused about what had prompted him to reach out, but as soon as I saw his sweet smile and the twinkle in his eyes, I just felt happy to be with him. There wasn't a moment of awkwardness or pretense during the game, but I was thrown by his sudden reappearance and still reeling from the heartbreak I had felt in Hawaii. As we walked back through the parking lot, I felt emboldened by how lovely it felt to be in step with him, reconnected and by his side.

"Steve, you know I'm not interested in another dress rehearsal."

He stopped walking and looked right at me. "I understand."

Wow, I thought, shocked at his confident answer. *May as well go for the gold.*

"And . . . I want to have children."

"Well. Okay, then," he said.

In 1986, we got engaged. He threw an extravagant party at the Sherman House, an elegant little hotel in Pacific Heights. It was December, and we told everybody that it was just a holiday gathering, though he had already proposed to me privately. Steve always had champagne taste, even though, at times, he had a Budweiser budget. For this occasion, he made sure everyone was drinking Krug Grande Cuvée champagne. He got up to make a toast and proposed again in front of all of our family and friends.

My political career had sped up to an exciting clip as well. In 1986, midway through my second term as a supervisor, I rolled the dice and ran for the California State Assembly, a leap Steve supported. In the primary I ran against Mike Nevin, the party's chosen candidate, a former police inspector and the mayor of Daly City. Willie Brown—the powerful assembly Speaker, who later became the mayor of San Francisco—told his broad base of influential allies to back Nevin. Nevin was also the brother-in-law of an assemblyman, so he had a tremendous amount of reach and support in the Bay Area. Nonetheless, by March, I and my growing band of volunteers had a fourteen-point lead in the polls, and the election was three months away. At that point Brown and his team threw everything at me: they bused in staffers from Sacramento and spread word among all the legislators and special interest groups not to support me. Speaker Brown felt I was too independent. It was a tough race. Steve wasn't particularly political, but he was by my side offering devotion and encouragement at the end of every day, which meant a great deal, especially as I was trying to navigate my way through fierce opposition. Still, it was a stressful time. It's never easy to have your character attacked on a public scale, to be bullied by someone who has the support of the establishment, or to have your views discredited by powerful sources. While that type of scrutiny comes with political office, the public applies a far more critical standard to a female politician running for office. I learned to accept empty criticism for what it was, and to use the opposition's bullying as an incentive to fuel my determination.

As the primary race neared its end, we were neck and neck, but my campaign was out of funds and I needed to get the last of my literature printed and mailed. It was too late in the primary to raise extra money, so I made the decision to walk into a bank in Burlingame and take out a loan against my condo—the condo my parents had put the down payment on when I'd returned from Guyana. I still vividly remember the loaded anxiety of walking around with a check for fifty thousand dollars, thinking, *I'm thirty-six years old and have just gone in to hock fifty grand on this election . . . What on earth am I going to do if I lose?* That risk was definitely not in keeping with the lessons of my prudent parents, who would never have gambled their only asset on a wholly uncertain future. I was in unfamiliar territory, but I'd been in a situation where I couldn't guarantee that the next day would come, and I felt ready to put everything I could behind this bid for office. It was a fretful decision, but we got the literature out on time.

The night of the primary arrived, and well into the evening the race was so close that neither candidate could celebrate; it was totally unclear who had won. Some wonderful people came out to support me that night, including Mayor Dianne Feinstein and other local officials. My stable of loyal friends and staff were by my side the whole time. It was a high-intensity evening, with hope surging, only to be deflated, only to blow up again. I steeled myself for victory, then defeat, then victory, then defeat, and eventually everyone had to leave without knowing for certain if our efforts had paid off. I went home that night to my mort-gaged condo, hoping I hadn't risked everything and lost.

A sleepless night later, it was finally announced that, out of forty thousand votes, the margin of victory was less than five hundred, in my favor. Even with the tentative victory announced, the outcome still wasn't confirmed for another two or three days. With the recounts in, it was finally official: I had won by little more than 1 percent of the vote, and while I still had a general election to win, the decidedly Democratic district secured my likely election to the state assembly. Six months later, I became the newly elected member of the California State Assembly—the same seat held by Leo Ryan when I had interned in his office sixteen years prior. I now had the job that I never thought I had the ability to win.

I was so proud. That was a big year for me, both personally and professionally, and I was heartened that my beloved grandma was alive to witness my campaign victory and know that I was engaged to a man I loved. She passed away later that month, peacefully, on Christmas Eve. Her fierce, devoted spirit—the same one that drove me to stand up and keep fighting for my life—has continued to serve as a guiding force through all the major touch points of my life.

Steve and I were married on August 8, 1987, during an assembly recess, at a magical ceremony in Sonoma County. Our reception colors were Wimbledon's green and purple. Kathleen and Katy were my bridesmaids, in lavender dresses. Steve was late to the wedding, which didn't surprise a single one of the two hundred fifty family members and friends who were already there. He apparently drove across the Golden Gate Bridge, honking his horn, holding a bottle of corked champagne out the window, shouting to the traffic that he was late for his wedding and to clear out of his way. He had a flair for the dramatic.

I had known since our first "date" that Steve was big on his fine wine. He had placed the highest bid to win a bottle of 1865 Volnay Santenots at an auction, and we saved it for the sacramental wine. The bottle itself was a work of art, with a label inked in black calligraphy and a cork sealed with red wax. We had become very good friends with our priest, Father Dan Keohane. As Father Dan blessed the wine and took the first sip, Steve leaned over to me and muttered under his breath, "I can't believe *he* gets the first sip of *that* wine," reducing me to quiet giggles. We not only shared the wine with all the guests who received communion that day, we also took it with us, drinking a little on our flight to Italy for our honeymoon, and finally finishing it off on a gondola in Venice. We'd made our way back to the fairy tale and were living it.

Pretty immediately, Steve and I wanted to start a family, but there were potential complications. One of the bullets from Guyana was still lodged in my pelvis, and my body had been through a lot of trauma. Our surprise and amazement were off the charts when, a few months after we got married, there was a blue strip on my home pregnancy test. Our life together seemed to be charmed, stretching before me exactly as I never could have dreamed.

I knew that I was going to stay in office, but in those days there was no road map to help women who wanted to balance being a mother with legislative work. We had to make it up as we went, ordering two of everything to create dual homes for our son—we had found out we would be having a boy—at our homes in South San Francisco and Sacramento. The birth went smoothly, relatively speaking, and especially considering the difficulties that the bullet in my pelvis could have caused during birth. Steve sat calmly in the room reading the paper as I was having contractions. My physical therapist who worked with me after Guyana had become a close friend, so she stepped in as my Lamaze coach, standing beside me and guiding me through the labor. After the fact, I was bewildered that Steve, an emergency-room doctor, hadn't urged me to get an epidural. Natural childbirth was very popular at the time, but there I was in the hospital with my friend encouraging me to breathe it out and pant in rhythm, which paled in comparison to the drugs that could have taken a huge amount of the edge off. At the end of it all, our beautiful son, Jackson, was born, completely healthy. I had the miraculous experience of breastfeeding my son for the first time, and then Steve dipped his finger in a glass of champagne and gave Jackson a tiny taste. It was July 1988, and—though our lives were filled to the brim—we couldn't have been happier.

I was the first California legislator to give birth while in office, which helped point me to an issue that needed to be addressed: the absence of a maternity leave for legislators. The Family and Medical Leave Act—a federal law that guarantees up to twelve workweeks of unpaid leave without the threat of losing one's job—did not pass for another five years. Instead, I took my accrued vacation time as maternity leave, which meant I was back to work within a few weeks. The office was understanding, but that didn't make the first day I left my newborn with his babysitter much easier. And although I was lucky enough to have the means to hire childcare, I still brought Jackson to the office with me for a month or so—I even held meetings with my staff where I had to cover up and breastfeed while we were discussing legislation. I was determined to continue serving in public office, but even more determined to be as good a mother as possible. It wasn't always easy to balance the two, but I found motherhood and my legislative work incredibly rewarding. There are plenty of people, then and now, who suggest that you cannot have both. In reality, having a mother in the legislature spotlighted new issues beyond parental leave that hadn't previously been discussed. I carried legislation on mandatory car seats and booster seats and how long kids legally had to be in them, as well as child-safety laws around things like fencing pools and recalling cribs that weren't safe. I passed a bill establishing that the proceeds from vanity license plates would go toward child-abuse prevention and child-safety programs. Most of those bills had not been introduced before, but they were each given due attention because of my new status as a mother. That's just one of the reasons why it's so important to encourage people from a range of backgrounds and circumstances to join the ranks of our government officials. If we don't have diverse representation, simple needs will be overlooked, and our legislation will never be as far reaching as it needs to be.

Those first years in office as a mother also helped me realize that using my own personal issues to inform my political life was a powerful impetus. In a way, it made clearer what drove Congressman Ryan on some of those daring missions—personal experience brings a clarity that nothing else can replace. And once I had it, I wasn't just more educated about an issue, I also felt a deeper responsibility to use that personal experience and awareness when advocating for my constituents.

The influence of personal experience has inspired me on more issues than just those that parenthood brought to my attention. For forty years, I have lived in a body that offers a daily reminder of the trauma of gun violence. I've held a fierce position advocating for commonsense prevention for just as long. In 1989, I was advised by well-meaning colleagues not to challenge the NRA, as it would bring a certain end to my political career. At that point, the NRA had not infiltrated the state legislature as much—they did not own our politicians as they do now in Congress. But the NRA has been powerful for quite some time and was very much opposed to any restriction, citing it as a violation of the Constitution. Against my colleagues' advice, I coauthored legislation to ban assault weapons in California. An assault weapon, such as the AR-15 that killed seventeen teenagers and teachers in Florida in 2018, is one that gives shooters more firepower than any police officer who may be in a position to stop the situation. There is no reason for civilians to buy and sell these weapons—no hunter needs an assault weapon to shoot Bambi. The ban on assault weapons was the toughest antigun legislation in the United States at the time, just as it would be today, shamefully.

I remember how my heart raced as I stood up at my desk on the floor of the state assembly to help present the bill. I had worked hard to make an airtight case and spent weeks crafting and refining my statement. One of my Republican colleagues who was against the bill (and unaware of my past) interrupted my statement.

"Ms. Speier, I have a question for you. Have you ever *shot* an assault weapon?" He did little to hide his condescension as he repeated, "Have *you* ever shot one?"

"No, Assemblyman," I responded. "But let me ask *you* a question: Have you ever been shot at point-blank range *by* an assault weapon?"

The room went absolutely silent. "Well *I* have and I can show you a lot of scars." I sat back down, breathing heavily.

The bill flew off the floor with overwhelming support, and Governor George Deukmejian, a Republican, signed it. Over fifty models of firearms were now banned in the state. It was the nation's first tough statewide legislation banning assault weapons, and one of the pinnacles of my career, a moment when I was able to use my personal tragedy to prevent—in some small way—the potential for others to endure anything similar. California remains among the few states that's tough on assault weapons, though it's all too easy for anybody to hop over the border, go to a gun show, or simply order one online. We're making progress every day, but it's not enough.

At the time, however, it felt like a rare moment of triumph in gun-violence prevention, for both Republicans and Democrats, adding to a time in my life that felt like a blessed collection of moments. I had a gorgeous one-year-old son who made my heart expand by the day; a sweet, loving husband who challenged me and whom I adored; and friends who kept me laughing. I was fulfilling my promise to devote myself to public service and witnessing real change. Everything I had yearned for, that I thought I'd never have, was opening up before me. But Guyana had also taught me not to take anything for granted. Not my health, not the person standing next to me, not a moment in time. That lesson, too, would soon be reinforced.

Chapter Seven

ENDINGS AND BEGINNINGS

In my life, I have been blessed with extraordinary love, and brought to my knees by shattering loss. When I returned from Guyana, I decided that life gives everybody their share of misfortune; mine had just come early in life and was a pretty extreme dose. I was wrong: life is not always fair. Life is just whatever you get. And while Guyana delivered incomparable trauma, it was not the worst day of my life.

The joy of having a family brought a whole new dimension to my existence. Watching my son grow and making space to care for him gave me my greatest moments of personal fulfillment. It was not an easy journey. While motherhood is an ineffable blessing, it is also the heaviest responsibility. Steve and I knew we wanted a second child. After Jackson, we optimistically tried for another. We were surprised, again, with a positive pregnancy test in 1990. I went in for what was going to be an early amnio at ten weeks. Steve and Jackson were both in the room with me as the cool gel was placed on my belly and the technician started moving the probe around. Words can't capture what it feels like for that expectancy of sound to be met by silence. They tried again but I already knew the truth. They couldn't find a heartbeat. Steve squeezed my hand and told me it would be fine. There's no comfort to be had when you've learned that you've lost a life that was growing inside of you, that you were waiting for, wanting. I kept it together for Jackson, but was inconsolable once we got home. "We'll try again" was all Steve could say. The loss of a baby, even if it's the size of a poppy seed in utero, is an indescribable loss. When people say you can try again, I appreciate it's an attempt at offering solace, but it feels like a dagger. It accentuates that the life that could have been did not survive. It's not a disposable thing; it's not a venture that you have the opportunity to redo. The grief I felt was crippling. I was so lucky to have Steve and Jackson to keep my spirits up, while work gave me the reasons I needed to get out of bed.

I got pregnant again in 1991. We were thrilled, though cautious, but we made it past the first twelve weeks and told all of our friends and family that we were planning for the arrival of our second child. We had already started discussing names and figuring out the logistics of two children, given our demanding careers. Four months into the pregnancy, Steve and I went for a jog, then he left to go to the hospital for work while I lay down for a nap. It had just started drizzling outside. As I was lying there, I could feel that something was wrong inside my belly. I called my ob-gyn to say that I felt like the fetus was slipping down, and he told me I needed to come in right away. Because of weak cervical tissue, the fetus had prematurely moved from the uterus and into the vagina. A friend picked me up and took me right to the hospital, where they harnessed me to a bed that positioned me with my legs in the air and my head down, in an attempt to get the fetus to slide back into the uterus. Had that been successful, they would have then sealed up my cervix. I spent the entire night in that position, crying the whole time. Steve arrived first thing the next morning, after his shift. I was sitting up in my drab gown when the doctor returned to the room with the kind of solemn look that you never want to see on your doctor's face. There was nothing further to be done. The fetus would not survive. I felt like I was losing a part of my soul. I had let myself believe another beautiful child was on the way, but I was wrong. Steve held me close.

Not only were we experiencing an unspeakable sense of loss, but with more anguish than I could imagine, I had to abort my pregnancy out of medical necessity. The crushing procedure, throughout which I was again sobbing, required dilating the cervix in order to extract the fetus. Ignorant or vindictive opponents have attacked that procedure—one of the great tragedies of my life—as a "partial-birth abortion."

That loss was among the darkest, lowest moments of my life, and one which I'd sooner compartmentalize and forget. It would have lasting effects, both on my heart and on my career. Not long after, I was home watching the Senate Judiciary Committee confirmation hearing of Clarence Thomas, who had been nominated for the Supreme Court. Anita Hill was testifying before an all-white male Judiciary Committee about the sexual harassment she had endured from Clarence Thomas when they were working for the Equal Employment Opportunity Commission. She was clear and honest about behaviors she had suffered under her former boss, and I found her testimony courageous; it rang true with so many experiences I had had in my life. I watched, incensed, as senator after senator questioned Anita Hill's veracity and tried to discredit her experience. It was so frustrating that I threw my slippers at the TV.

That moment felt like a clarion call. I was still raw from my personal loss, and I was furious at the way women were asked to endure so much—to put up with unfair treatment and insufficient laws to support our needs—yet were given such little support. I immediately got to work, ramping up my campaign to ensure safe work environments free of unwanted sexual advances. I carried legislation that became law in California requiring all businesses to provide employees with a pamphlet explaining their right to be free from harassment in the workplace. I called on the Speaker of the assembly to require all its members to participate in yearly sexual harassment prevention programs. He agreed and the requirement was adopted for California.

Then about two decades later, on a defining evening in February of 2011, a number of my Democratic colleagues and I were alarmed about Congressman Mike Pence's move to defund Planned Parenthood. With Congress in session, I listened in growing shock as one of our other Republican colleagues stood up in support of the bill. A congressman from New Jersey casually labeled the procedure as "fetal murder," and went on to malign women who received medically necessary abortions. What sickened me the most was that he picked up a book and started reading about the procedure, including details like cutting off the limbs of the fetus. That's what really sent me into orbit. *How dare you?* I knew that I had to say something, not just to correct his smug misconceptions, but on behalf of the millions of women who have suffered, and continue to suffer—there's no other word for it—through the procedure that he was degrading by callously reading from a book.

I was set to speak after him, and I left my prepared notes behind me as I approached the podium. Trembling with nerves and rage, I informed the congressman that he had put my stomach in knots—not merely because he had no idea what he was talking about, but because I was one of the women whom he had just described. I had suffered through what he was calling "murder," and the idea that there was anything cavalier about my decision and my shattering loss was preposterous.

As I walked off the floor that night, I was still visibly shaking. Representative John Lewis came up to me with tears in his eyes. "Jackie, that's one of the most powerful speeches I've ever heard on the floor," he said. He proceeded to share a devastating childhood memory of seeing his mom walk his aunt down the stairs of their home. His aunt's nightgown was soaked in blood. His mother rushed her to the hospital, but Congressman Lewis never saw his aunt again.

That same night in Washington, one of my female colleagues whispered in my ear, "That was so brave of you. I never could have done it." She had undergone a similar procedure, but was too intimidated or humiliated to admit as much. When that impromptu speech went viral, I received thousands of letters, calls, and emails from women around the country, many of whom echoed my colleague's experience: they had been through the same thing, but had never said a word. The evidence of how many women suffer in silence was staggering. That devastating day in 1991, one I wish I had never experienced, gave me the necessary courage and perspective to speak out—louder and more often—on behalf of the masses of women who couldn't do the same. It also made me realize just how much I could use the assembly floor as a megaphone, to address the silent or silenced.

Following my second miscarriage, Steve, Jackson, and my friends kept me resilient. While I didn't feel my body was ready to try for another pregnancy, we wanted to grow our family. We had discussed adoption in the past, but hadn't started the process. In June, Steve called me from the emergency room, where a young woman had just given birth to a baby she didn't want to keep. We didn't have to discuss matters for very long. After completing the requisite paperwork, we were cleared to adopt this remarkable gift of a baby boy, toward whom I instantly felt the fierce bond of motherhood. We named him Austin Parker.

The love was immediate for both of us. We were ecstatic, and I was attached from the first night as I watched him sleep. It's no exaggeration to say I fell deeper in love each time I held him. A little over a week later, we were in Sacramento, trying to get the budget passed. I brought Austin with me onto the floor and was there until very late—it was probably one or two in the morning by the time we finally voted. I remember the complete joy of holding this beautiful sleeping infant in my arms on the assembly floor. When we got home, Jackson was asleep. I put Austin down in his crib, then told the babysitter, "I desperately need to get some rest. If Austin needs a feeding, would you mind giving him a bottle? I'm going to try to sleep until eight or so."

At seven o'clock the babysitter shook me awake. "I'm sorry, but Steve's on the phone. He said he needs to speak with you right now."

I rolled over and picked up the phone. "I was trying to get a little sleep," I grumbled.

"Jackie, it's the mother. She wants the baby back. They're coming up to Sacramento today."

I couldn't understand. He repeated himself, but I still couldn't register what he was saying. He later explained that Austin's birth mother had never told her own mother that she was pregnant, or that she had given birth to a son. When his grandmother found out, she insisted that they get the baby back. A few hours later, the two women arrived at our home. They didn't have a car seat, or diapers, or any clothes for him: nothing. Robotically, without letting myself feel, I gave them all of the things that we had bought for Austin. Anger and frustration would come, but the most present emotion I felt then was just a crushing sense of loss. I kissed his little head goodbye and watched them drive away, knowing I would never see him again.

Austin's mother had every right to take him. I was entirely aware of that. In California, the birth parent had the right to claim their child back for up to six months. Given how intensely connected I had felt after ten days, I cannot imagine what it would have felt like to part with him after months of being his mother. I later passed legislation changing the law from one hundred eighty days to one hundred twenty days. I didn't want any adopting parent to feel the sorrow I was feeling. I couldn't believe that we had lost our miracle baby so quickly. Blessedly, I knew I had to stay upright for Jackson. But a wellspring of hurt gathered inside of me from the moment they drove away, one that I had no idea how to hold back. The dam broke when I was driving back to San Francisco, once Jackson had fallen asleep in the back. I called

Steve, crying. "Why do these bad things keep happening to us? I don't understand. It's just not fair! I—"

"Now wait a minute," he stopped me. "We have a wonderful, perfect child. We have each other. We have our health. And we can try again." He was right. We had more than our share of blessings, and I knew that fairness was not a reasonable barometer. I didn't know about trying again, however. I was forty-two years old. I had endured two miscarriages, and I would always have a bullet lodged in my pelvic region. At this point, the odds of expanding our family weren't looking great. I sighed.

"Okay," I said with a wary heart, "let's try again."

We went to the fertility specialist a couple of months later. I had already taken a number of tests. The specialist looked at my records and told us, without a great deal of tact or sensitivity, "Based on the age of your eggs and your medical history, you have a 10 percent chance of getting pregnant *with* in-vitro fertilization." The procedure would cost about ten thousand dollars. Steve and I agreed that it was impractical to go through all of that—hormone treatments and a potentially disappointing medical procedure—with the odds stacked so high against us. Together, we decided to close that chapter of our lives. We had our beautiful, growing son, a fabulous marriage, and thriving careers. I turned my energy back to politics and decided to run for secretary of state of California. It was 1993, and I began preparing for the upcoming race the following year.

A few months later, swept back into the chaos of running for office, I hardly noticed that my cycle was a little off. I was campaigning statewide, and my free moments were devoted to my family. That time of the month came and went, and I just got on with my work. After a good while, however, I realized that I was actually several weeks late. I couldn't be pregnant naturally, I thought, so I didn't bother getting my hopes up.

December arrived, and I was home with Jackson. Steve was working the night shift, and I had a little extra time to indulge the niggling possibility by checking my calendar to calculate just how late I was. Our babysitter was there, so at eleven at night I spontaneously went to get a pregnancy test—I had taken so many, it wouldn't really mean anything to get another negative result. I drove to Walgreens and bought the test that had turned the wrong color more times than I could count. I paced around the bathroom as I waited the two minutes for the result, then carefully picked up the test strip. I stared at it for a while, stunned. I couldn't believe it. I finally pulled myself together to call Steve at the hospital.

"Honey, guess what?"

"What?"

"I . . . think I might be pregnant."

He paused. "What was it, immaculate conception?"

We laughed, equally dumbfounded, but he told me to come to the hospital immediately and get my blood taken so we could be sure. It was almost midnight but I drove down, had my blood drawn, and went home. Steve called at around seven in the morning, and I bolted up and grabbed the phone.

"You know what? You *are* pregnant!"

It didn't seem real. I was cautiously excited. After everything we had endured, after the devastation of the miscarriages, after losing Austin, and after our final discussion and decision to move on, what were the odds that I would have gotten pregnant naturally, at age forty-three, by accident? The doctors recognized the unlikelihood and deemed it a very high-risk pregnancy, especially with what was medically referred to as my "incompetent cervix." Leave it to men to choose that name for such a devastating condition! I was likely to be on bed rest when I neared my due date. That additional anxiety made it obvious that I was not in ideal shape to run for statewide office.

Early in January 1994, I announced in the governor's press conference room that I would no longer be running for secretary of state due to my high-risk pregnancy. A reporter shouted out, "Ms. Speier, you're a feminist. Isn't this a blow to feminism?"

What rock did you just come out from under? I thought. I cleared my throat and said, "I don't think you understand. There is a life at risk, and I'm not going to do anything to raise that risk level." That was my personal choice. It is a tough decision that many women—feminists or not—must grapple with, but when it came down to it, I wanted this baby. I loved my work, but my personal priority was the child inside of me. The idea that any one woman's choice around her pregnancy and career can or should set back an entire gender is preposterous—but it's an attitude that women in all fields continue to deal with today. I put my career on pause with every intention of returning stronger and prepared to deal with anything. I geared up to run for reelection for the state assembly.

A few weeks into the pregnancy, I noticed a little bit of bleeding. I got in bed, terrified that I was going to lose another baby. Later that evening, Jackson and Steve walked into the bedroom, and our five-year-old stood there with his hands behind his back and a cute little impish smile on his face. Steve nudged him closer to the bed. Jackson stepped up and presented me with a long-stemmed red rose. It made me so happy, I nearly wept. We all laughed instead. This was the life I wanted.

A day or two later, I was on my way to Sacramento to give a speech to the California Bankers Association. My district director, Judy Bloom, was driving us through a torrential downpour when I got the phone call.

"Jackie," my secretary began, in a strange voice, "there's been a call from the San Mateo police. Steve's been in an accident."

Judy turned the car around immediately to drive back. I called the hospital, and they put me through to a friend of Steve's, the same surgeon who had operated on Grandma's gallbladder.

"What happened?" I asked, feeling a slight wave of panic.

"Jackie. It's . . . it's not good. You should just get here as soon as you can."

I hadn't realized how serious it was until I heard the quiet devastation in his voice. We sped to Mills Hospital in San Mateo, where they left me in the waiting room with no further information. I tried to be patient, but finally I couldn't take it any longer.

"Let me see him," I demanded.

He was in the ICU. They had done everything they could. Though his body was still warm, Steve was brain dead.

Steve had been broadsided by a young man who had driven in that downpour, even though he knew his car had faulty brakes. He ran a red light at the intersection of Poplar and San Mateo Drive and plowed right into Steve's car. What was all the more twisted was that this young man worked at an auto parts shop. The details didn't compute at the time. It seemed too senseless, too reckless to be true.

Word spread like wildfire among the physicians. It wasn't his hospital, but when he was hit and they were bringing him in, the police had repeated, "He's one of our own; he's one of our own." A doctor there was trying to get me to pull the plug immediately. But I just couldn't. The whole scene didn't compute. Nothing made sense. The lights, the tubes, the machines. Everybody was waiting on me. All I could do was nod yes or shake my head no. I was in a genuine state of shock, staring down horrific emotional pain, slipping through it like quicksand, with nothing to hold on to, and nobody there to guide me through this nightmare. My soul mate was gone, and part of me had gone with him. He was being kept alive by artificial means, and they were waiting on me to end it.

I shut off my heart and tried to figure out what needed to be done. Jackson. I needed to pick up Jackson from kindergarten. I had to call Steve's brother, who was in Oregon, so he could fly down and pay his respects. I went to pick up Jackson from school, and we drove back to the hospital. He was dressed in his little karate uniform. I took his hand, and we walked into the ICU together and stood in front of Steve's body, in the same way that the two of them had come and stood by my bed with the red rose. "Jackson," I said quietly, "you need to say goodbye to your daddy." He didn't understand what was happening, but he kissed him and looked back up at me, then asked if he could go to karate. "Of course," I told him, and a friend took him away.

Steve's brother, Ken, got on the first flight out and made it down a few hours later to say his goodbyes. I called Father Dan, who rushed to the hospital to give Steve his last rites. After that, everyone was just standing there, waiting for me to make perhaps the most difficult decision of my life. I kissed my husband goodbye. His lips were warm. Then I nodded to the doctor, and walked out of the room.

The days that followed were a numbing combination of emptiness and frenzy. Friends gathered around to support me. My friend Sharon Kime, a wonderful, deep soul, was in Sacramento when she heard about Steve's accident. She immediately got in her car and drove down through that same torrential downpour to help me navigate those first few days. Sharon had lost her husband the year before, so she understood firsthand how paralyzing that initial shock could be. She was among those who were especially helpful, bringing me food and taking care of details that never would have occurred to me. I don't know what I would have done without them. I don't know how I would have gotten out of bed, let alone planned a funeral. I sat in Starbucks with one of my girlfriends, going over all of the details. In a daze, I watched people walk by us, get in the line, buy their coffee, and move on with their lives. Meanwhile, my life was in shambles. Why was everyone else's life so normal? It was like seeing Kathleen in her pilot's uniform at the Shock Trauma Center in Baltimore all over again. And there I was, just this mass of matter that couldn't function. This time, I truly felt like my world had come to an end.

Once Steve was gone, I had to decide where to bury him. Father Dan and I went to visit Holy Cross, a well-regarded Catholic cemetery where my grandparents were buried, and where my parents had already bought their plots. It seemed like a fitting place, but I found it too depressing, too foggy. I imagined my kids going to his grave and feeling miserable about their father. I didn't want that; more importantly, he would never have wanted that. I wanted a place that felt uplifting somehow, where they could go and celebrate the fun-loving man that Steve was. Father Dan then took me up to Skylawn Memorial Park, which overlooked Half Moon Bay and the endless Pacific Ocean. I looked out and thought, *This is where Steve wants to be.* So I bought his plot immediately and had a tombstone created that read:

STEVEN K. SIERRA. Beloved husband, father, son, brother, friend, and physician to the needy. He inspired us, taught us how to love, and lived life to the fullest.

Above the epitaph we had a mountain range etched, because Steve always used to say, "It's Sierra, like the mountains."

At the funeral, the church was overflowing with people. The Mercy High School chorale came to sing. And Father Dan, who had married us, presided. Steve was dressed in his tennis clothes. Jackson and I chose items to place in the casket; Jackson chose a rock, and I included a love letter that I had written. I knew Steve would have wanted people to smile when they thought of him, so we put a tennis racket on top of the casket, and a red rose from Jackson.

Losing Steve was more traumatic than anything that had ever happened to me, and there were times I presumed I would never overcome it. Alone in the bedroom we had shared, I was haunted, devastated by what had been and what could have been had he lived. I was devoid of energy, joy, resources, or a will to live. What would it mean to bring the baby I was carrying into a world where she would know no father? How would I cope with the confluence of single parenthood and my own crippling grief? What kind of a mother would I be, scarred as I was? These questions and doubts churned in my mind, keeping me awake at night and following me as I robotically went through the motions of each day.

Steve had recently canceled his life insurance in order to save some money because we were paying three mortgages—our homes in Burlingame and Sacramento, and our newly purchased dream house in Hillsborough—so my anguish was compounded as I tried to work through a financial nightmare. There was something about him canceling it that had nagged at me, but he had assured me that it was all fine, and that we would reinstate the insurance when we sold the house in Burlingame. I had always known Steve wasn't great with money, but he had brought me so much joy and love—areas in which my life had been deficient—that his lack of financial judgment seemed a small imperfection for a man I loved. But with him gone, that burden felt crushing. A few days after the funeral, I sat around my dining room table with my accountant, an attorney friend, a Realtor friend, and a couple of bright and supportive girlfriends. They were all there to help me try to piece together a logistical plan to pull myself out of this financial hellhole. My parents couldn't help at this point; they just gave me sobering advice. I sold the house in Sacramento and the house in Hillsborough, and when I was working in the capital, I stayed with my brother. I had to put our dream house, the place Steve and I had just bought, where we envisioned growing our family, on the market. It was the recession, so there was no likelihood of selling our home for the price that we had paid for it. But I had no choice. There was no way I could make the payments—I was walking on a knife's edge and only very narrowly avoiding bankruptcy. I remember sitting in the backyard during the open house while a stream of strangers wandered through, assessing it. I can still feel that hollowed-out desperation.

Blessedly, we hadn't managed to sell our previous house in Burlingame yet. Jackson, the baby inside of me, and I were able to move back to the house. That was another set of circumstances in which, I believe, some form of divine intervention was involved. But I hated feeling so helpless. My parents visited at least twice a week. A few months in, my dad sat down in my bedroom and asked how I was doing. The dam holding back my grief collapsed. I told him I didn't want to go on. I didn't know how I was going to manage. He had always encouraged me to stand up for myself and to carry on, no matter the obstacle before me. In a rare showing of German stoic insistence, he looked me in the eye and said, "Jackie, get over it. It has been three months."

I was outraged. He had no concept of my anguish. I yelled at him to leave and we didn't speak for weeks. But he was right, and somewhere inside, I knew it. I needed to reflect strength and hope to my five-year-old son. I had to pick him up from kindergarten with love to give. I had to nurture the baby in my womb, a baby Steve and I had been so thrilled to have on the way. Feeling sorry for myself was robbing my children of the energy and caring they deserved. But I needed more time before I could completely "get over it." There are chasms of grief that can't be willed away. Some bullets never leave the body. But even when we can't get over it, we still have to move forward. And so, tentatively, I started to take my first steps.

In those first months, I leaned heavily into my faith. I prayed a lot. And it was faith that powered my belief that if I got out of bed, if I could just manage that forward movement, I would be able to handle the circumstances of the day. That was more complicated when I was officially placed on bed rest. I had always used work as therapy in tough times, so being in bed alone with my thoughts was incredibly difficult. I still negotiated legislative bills over the phone, but that never felt as active and involved as I liked to be. At that point, I felt I had my wits about me enough to think, *All right, here are your choices. You can wallow. Does this feel good? Do you want to stay with it forever? Or you can stop feeling sorry for yourself and trust that you will get through this, just as you've gotten through every tragedy in your life, as untold numbers of people dealing with untold hardships are getting through their days.*

While part of me still bristles at my father's lack of sensitivity, I understand what he meant. We can stay astride with life only if we negotiate the inevitable obstacles that obstruct our path. Grief is a frightening obstacle. It was tempting to lie down in the road and succumb to it. But I had legacies to honor: Grandma's determination, Dad's love, Mom's grit, Leo's intrepid spirit, Steve's joie de vivre. Most importantly, I had Jackson, and the baby inside of me. No, I would not yield. That was not the plan for me.

The following summer, our beautiful daughter, Stephanie Katelin Sierra, named for her father, was born. Steve and I had decided on naming her Sabrina, but my dear friend Linda Dean—a massage therapist who came by to give me massages after Steve died and then when I was on bed rest—kept referring to her as Stephanie. After Linda left one day I thought, *Of course, she should be named for her father*. Her middle name was in honor of Katy and Linda, but it also represented how exceptionally supportive all of my friends were throughout those months as I waited to give birth, and how deeply invested in Stephanie's life they were.

So when the nurse asked me who I wanted to have in the room with me for the actual birth, I couldn't choose. I told her whoever wanted to be present was welcome to come in. There must have been fifteen to twenty people inside of the hospital room while I was giving birth. We had a photograph of Steve and a little split of Krug Grand Cuvée champagne beside my bed. Nancy, Jackson's half sister from Steve's previous marriage, drove him to the hospital. When they came into the room, Jackson continued his father's tradition and gave his baby sister a little sip of Grand Cuvée off his finger. Looking around at my friends and family, holding my miraculous baby girl and smiling at Jackson, I was overwhelmed with awe. The people in that delivery room had kept me afloat throughout what otherwise would have been a crippling downward spiral. They had helped me come to terms with the most gut-wrenching reminder that I could not waste my time here. I knew that the world was waiting, with extraordinary opportunities to offer, as soon as I learned how to open my heart again . . . and as long as I got myself out of bed to meet them.

Chapter Eight

WHEN ONE DOOR CLOSES . . .

Just as definitively as I believe that failure paves a route toward success, I know that the end of one opportunity, or of one great love, makes all the more room for the beginning of another. Helen Keller said, "When one door of happiness closes, another opens; but often we look so long at the closed door that we do not see the one that has been opened for us." I don't know how long it would have taken me to stop staring at the door that closed on my life with Steve, nor can I fathom how much harder it would have been for me to overcome the challenges and unexpected pivots of my life, without the advice and love from my friends.

Friendship has been as essential to my survival as water, or that potent rum in Guyana. Shared laughter, loyal counsel, little notes of encouragement—those connections have made my journey not just bearable, but illuminated by joy. My girlfriends have seen me at my weakest and, in those moments, embraced me that much tighter, helping me navigate through political loss, relationships that have left me blindsided, and bewildering mazes of grief.

Like most people, I've endured spans of time when I felt like life was dealing only hardship. But there were always means of coping. I coped with Steve's death and the aftermath, while raising a six-year-old son and an infant daughter, by leaning on my friends. There were dining-room-table gatherings that helped me evade bankruptcy, the nights when I needed help taking care of my children, and the late-night conversations when I just needed to fill the void of silence. I called on them many times, and they were always there in a flash.

The year after Steve's death, my dear friend Jan Yanehiro lost her husband. We were acquaintances at the time, but she—as a TV reporter and host of her own show—had interviewed me for many of the Guyana anniversaries. Her son, J.B., and Jackson were the same age, and they played in the same soccer league. They would have games and tournaments on Saturdays where Jan and I would show up, both late every time, without fail. We'd both be dressed in suits (and I don't mean jogging ones) because we were both going full force with our careers at that time.

Jan had kindly offered to throw me a baby shower after Steve's death. That shower never happened because, tragically, her forty-six-year-old husband, John, was diagnosed with glioblastoma, the most aggressive form of brain cancer. He died six months later. In the same way that Sharon Kime had known exactly what I needed after Steve's death, I was able to pay the kindness forward to Jan. Having just gone through the process, I led her through what needed to be taken care of and when it had to be done. An early piece of advice to her, of the sort you can really only hear and laugh about with another widow, was to *charge* everything—the casket, the funeral plot, the gravestone, the reception, all of it—because those charges would yield plenty of air miles, which she could then use to take her kids on a vacation. She had her husband buried at Skylawn as well, overlooking Half Moon Bay in a plot on the same hill as Steve's. Jan has three children, so on the first Father's Day without either of our husbands, we took our kids to the cemetery for a picnic. Jan brought KFC, and her daughters, ten and twelve at the time, brought a boom box. We sat in the June sun, listening to music and playing with baby Stephanie, who was only

With Kevin and Pat Ryan, Leo's son and daughter who supported me during my first race for Congress.

Campaign literature from my first race to fill Leo Ryan's seat.

My father proudly standing in front of an early campaign sign. I'm surprised our budget allowed for the balloons!

Honoring Leo Ryan alongside members of his family at the ceremony in Washington, DC, to present Ryan with the posthumous Congressional Gold Medal in 1983.

My brother, Eric, and my grandmother outside our home in Burlingame, near Mercy High.

A family portrait, with my father, mother, and grandmother when she was living in my parents'
home.

Steve and me on our wedding day on August 8, 1987.

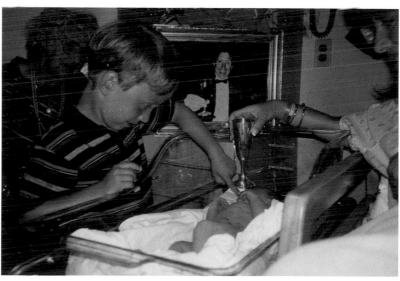

Jackson gives Stephanie her first taste of champagne with Mom, and my favorite photo of Steve looking on in the background, August 10, 1994.

Stephanie, me, and Jackson at his first Holy Communion, with Father Dan, who has been there for so many of the important days in my life.

Years later, Father Dan giving Stephanie her first Holy Communion.

With my mom by my side, announcing my 1998 bid for State Senate in front of the Inner Sunset flats she had purchased fifty years before.

With my close friends Deborah Stephens, Linda Dean, and Katy Lawson, who have seen me through the highs and lows in my life.

Queen Amidala, a golfer, and Disney's Belle. I still get excited about Halloween every year!

The Merry Widows Club during one of our winter gatherings.

Barry and me on our wedding day, October 13, 2001, in Carmel, California.

Barry in his true element, on a lake, with a fresh catch (that he's about to release back to the water).

The yoga girls celebrating the holidays with our annual ugly sweater competition.

Mom, still teaching her upholstery classes into her nineties. She was one of the hardest-working women I've ever known.

Barry, me, Jackson, and Stephanie at our log cabin, enjoying some family time.

At my desk in Washington, DC, catching up on correspondence with my constituents.

Frederica Wilson, me, Gabby Giffords, and Nancy Pelosi at the ceremony naming the House Democratic Cloakroom for Giffords and Leo Ryan. I was honored to stand with three powerful and extraordinary women that day.

One of Mom's original pin cushions along with her funeral mass program that I left behind when I visited Armenia for the centennial of the genocide.

Giving a speech at the Assault Weapons Ban press conference after the horrific Pulse nightclub shooting in 2016, surrounded by boxes of petitions.

The helmet that I keep in my office, signed by survivors of sexual assault in the military to remind me that between fifteen and twenty thousand service members are sexually assaulted every year.

Celebrating with a rally of strong, smart, capable women who know their worth after introducing a joint resolution that would finally allow for the ratification of the Equal Rights Amendment, February 1, 2017.

At the inauguration in 2017, where I proudly wore my pussy hat as a symbol of my dedication to women's rights, with Dave Loebsack of Iowa, Kathy Castor of Florida, and Andre Carson of Indiana.

Mark Wilson/Getty Images

An amazing group of Democratic congresswomen. Our numbers in Congress may be small, but we pack a powerful and growing punch. I am proud to stand among them.

ten months old and crawled around on the bright-green grass. The boys brought a Wiffle ball and bat, and asked us if they could use the gravestones as bases. Jan and I agreed that our husbands would have approved of the unorthodox playing field. We laughed and cried and laughed our way back through the anguish of the surreal scene, together. Even now, if ever I go to take flowers to Steve's grave, I'll lay a few on John's grave—and I know that Jan does the same.

Jan and I are united by more than our shared tragedy. We are both forward thinking, hopeful women, and one of our most important decisions together was to lift the shroud off our grief and start calling ourselves the Merry Widows. We wanted to continue the tradition of opening our arms to other widows. Initially, that meant bringing women food, taking them to lunch, advising them on how to maneuver through funeral arrangements, or simply being an understanding presence. Nearly twenty-five years later, our Merry Widows Club has grown into a robust support group. It's not a club that anybody would want to join, but it has been an incredible source of joy and relief for me.

At our lunches or dinners, liberated from trying to be upbeat or appropriate, we discuss everything from the agony of clearing out closets to the mundane paperwork required—who else wants to listen to you lament about having to order multiple death certificates for all the filings?—to what we put on top of our husbands' caskets. I had the tennis racket and rose; Jan put her husband's favorite Mrs. Fields chocolate chip cookies, poker chips, and photographs. Another one of our Merries confided that she had placed her husband's cell phone, fully charged, inside the casket . . . and that she had called and left him messages for months after. Macabre as that sounds, we can all laugh, relate, and confess to one another, often before ordering another round.

A dozen of us, give or take, still gather every few months. We celebrate major holidays—especially Valentine's Day—take trips to different cities, have adventures, learn new coping mechanisms, cry as much as we need to, and laugh a whole lot. As the years passed, the conversations shifted from "Which item of your husband's clothing did you keep?" to "What should I bring for my first weekend trip with this new guy? Pajamas? Silk nighties?"

Nobody can save us from the inevitable wells of sorrow that continue to open up from time to time. We have all lost our best friends, lovers, and soul mates. Nobody else can actually pick us up off the ground and keep us upright—that's up to each of us. But once we have gotten ourselves back on our feet, there's nothing like sitting down with true friends, sharing stories, and raising a glass to one another.

For seven years, I pressed on as a single working mom with two children. At work, my opponents often resented the hardline positions I took, particularly in fighting for women. In 1996, I talked about my medically necessary abortion on the floor, and a Republican colleague responded in a closed-door caucus afterward by commenting that "Jim Jones didn't finish the job." That was a particularly extreme, offensive case, but that kind of vitriol followed me. I'm not immune to the initial sting or shock of such comments, but having faced true disaster has made it easier to rebound from those petty comments and place naysayers and bullies in perspective. Slowly, I came to be respected in the California assembly for the amount of legislation my staff and I passed.

California term limits dictated that I had to give up my assembly seat in 1996, so I focused my sights on the California State Senate. I decided to honor Mom by announcing my candidacy in 1998 in front of the same flats on Irving Street that she had bought more than half a century prior. The neighborhood was in my district, which stretched from San Francisco through San Mateo County, and my mother was at the press conference. I'd love to think that, as she stood beside me and the homes she had toiled to buy, watching my announcement, she was marveling at what her years of hard work had yielded . . . but my mom was never one to marvel. More likely, she was hoping she wouldn't be late to her next class; she continued teaching upholstery until she was ninety-three years old.

The election was hard work, but comparatively less dramatic than those for the assembly. I won by a comfortable margin. In the Senate, I continued fighting the battles I had waged in the assembly, consistently reinforcing that a legislator has to be patient and dogged to pursue real change. One of my bills, which mandated that insurers cover birth control pills, the only class of drugs not covered on most prescription drug benefits, took four years to get signed into law. I ran into a series of obstacles and excuses and of course those opposed to it, but eventually it passed in part because Pfizer had introduced Viagra, which was instantly covered in prescription drug benefits. No one could argue that Viagra was less expensive to cover than contraceptive pills, so there was no reason for the exception. Pointing out that ridiculous misogyny— the willingness to cover a drug that treats men's impotence and not cover a drug that not only prevents unwanted pregnancies but also alleviates some painful symptoms of diseases like endometriosis—was how we got the bill passed and signed into law. We had to be creative and steadfast, and we had to take advantage of any such opportunity.

In the State Senate, I engaged in no shortage of clashes, but after the wrangling we'd all sit down together, roll up our sleeves, and find solutions that enabled us to get laws passed. That occasionally meant building coalitions across party lines with the strangest bedfellows, even colleagues who maintained policy positions that confounded me. But we were persistent, and all sides got their chance to speak. Every bill got a hearing; every issue was open to discussion and negotiation for the public record. Nobody had the power to bury a gun violence prevention bill, take a nap on immigration, or sweep major legislation under the rug and not vote on it. It was possible for me to get over three hundred bills signed into law, with the support of governors from both parties. These included the nation's strongest financial privacy law, legislation that became the gold standard of consumer protection, and laws that expanded women's access to reproductive health services and improved collection of delinquent child support payments. I led high-profile investigations of prison corruption, gender inequity in the University of California faculty, the steroid industry, and fraudulent government spending. Some of these fights lasted years; many were caustic; but they all happened. I was always given the opportunity to be heard. In turn, I was expected to hear out the other side—I trusted that that was how government worked at every level. In time, I would learn that I was wrong.

As a public servant my work is never finished, my to-do list never completed. That is even more true of being a mother. My devotion to both meant that my kids have made enormous sacrifices. Mixing parenthood with a hectic work life is exhausting for everybody, and when there's just one parent, it's especially hard. But Jackson and Stephanie were never short of love. In addition to my tight circles of friends, my parents lent a hand. They certainly weren't doting grandparents, like Grandma had been with me. But they pitched in and helped care for Stephanie and Jackson. My mom even taught Stephanie how to sew, and Stephanie enjoyed sitting and watching her grandmother's capable, weathered hands move swiftly across the fabric. She adored her grandpa, and of course the feeling was mutual. He called her his little Mickey Mouse.

A couple of years after Steve died, I started dating again. I didn't have the time, between work and home, but I was ready. I wanted to see what was out there, so I went on dates here and there. Stephanie was still quite young, and Jackson took it in stride. He even gave my various suitors spot-on nicknames like Psycho Doc and Bill Gates Wannabe, which always made me laugh and eased the disappointment when it didn't work out. I wanted my children to have a father, but it takes a certain type of man to be interested in a politician with two small children. Not only was I a public figure, I was a public figure who landed on local television whenever I was being argumentative or feisty, which was often. I was a lot to take on, but I also had a lot of love to give. My heart had begun to reopen, if cautiously.

One of my fellow Merries, Kathleen Alioto, is a big-hearted matchmaker. In 2000, she was traveling to Dublin with some friends and their investment consultant, Barry Dennis, whom she thought I might hit it off with. As they were sitting together on the plane, she asked him if he knew Jackie Speier.

"I know of her," he said.

"Would you like to go out with her? She is an amazing woman, and she's smart enough for you. I could arrange a meeting?"

"No, thank you," Barry answered immediately.

Surprised, she left it at that, but not for long. They landed early in Dublin, and the group went to see the Book of Kells at Trinity College. As Barry and Kathleen walked through the streets of Dublin, she couldn't help herself. "Are you *sure* you wouldn't like to meet Jackie?" she asked.

"You know, I'm an introvert, and I'm not that interested in politics. So I'm sure, but thank you."

Undeterred, she persisted, but finally had to let it go. He wasn't budging.

She saw him a few more times and used each occasion to push the issue a little further. Finally, after the fifth or sixth encounter, at an event back in San Francisco, she not so subtly suggested that he at *least* call me. "Yeah, okay, fine" was his not-so-enthusiastic response. She gave Barry my phone number and he called a few days later, as I was heading to the Sacramento airport to catch a plane. I was going to a friend's barbecue the following Saturday and asked if he would like to come as my guest. He agreed, but suggested we meet beforehand and have a glass of wine and get to know each other a little better.

A few days later Barry arrived to pick me up. I opened the door, and there he was in thick horn-rimmed glasses, wearing a plaid short-sleeved shirt. *Hmm,* I thought. *Perhaps not quite my type.* But he seemed very genuine over our conversation. It was obvious that he was a remarkably decent man. Barry and I went to the barbeque, but it was mobbed with public figures—judges, attorneys, and other politicos. I tried to stick with my date, but people kept pulling me away to network. Barry ended up standing around alone a lot.

After that, I figured it was over, as neither of us had really had that much fun at the event. But he got in touch and we decided to give it another try. On our second date, I learned a little more about his midwestern roots, and he told me—at length—about his true passion: fly-fishing. I later said to my friends, "Do *I* look like a fly fisherman? Or a fly fisherman's wife, for that matter?" But, lack of shared interests aside, there was something intriguing about Barry. He was totally different from the men of my past—to an extreme degree. I had always been drawn to the loud, gregarious, overtly charming, and—as it often seemed to turn out—quite unreliable types. That was not Barry. But there was something inexplicably lovely about his nature, and I knew I'd regret not giving it another shot. A few weeks later, we made plans to go on our third date to Moose's restaurant, a lively spot right in the Italian district of San Francisco. I launched into Twenty Questions with him.

"So, how many children do you have?" I asked.

"None."

"Oh. Well, how many times have you been married?"

"None."

"Engaged?"

"Never."

"Are you . . . gay?"

"No."

It was beyond me how an intelligent, good-looking, successful guy could reach fifty years old without getting married. Never one for subtlety, I questioned him about it, and our conversation got deeper and more personal than it had on our previous dates. Always one for subtlety, he was thoughtful with his responses—he said what he meant, and meant what he said. And though at times it required some dogged interrogation on my part, the more he shared, the more interested I became. I asked him about his work in the finance world. As complicated as his profession sounded, there was an altruistic undercurrent to his perspective, and he spoke with an attractive clarity about advising people to make sure that they were rewarded for the work they had done in their lives by retiring well. Without a trace of arrogance, he distilled convoluted concepts and made them easy to grasp. He was quietly perceptive; as he gradually let his guard down and our conversation began to flow organically, it became evident that he read people very well and was an astute observer of character. None of these were qualities I would have immediately assigned to my previous partners, nor were they on the list of traits I had ever sought out in men whom I'd dated. But they distinguished Barry and left me eager to learn more about him. Besides, I had been on enough rollercoaster rides. I craved steady, reliable ground and a genuine companion who would take my hand and share the journey with me.

We made plans to go on a trip to the wine country, but I first had a commitment to serve as an auctioneer at a Crohn's and colitis charity event in San Francisco. He offered to come along to the auction. At the podium, as I was auctioning a trip to New York, Barry, to my surprise, started bidding aggressively, and eventually bought it for a significant amount of money. "You know, you really didn't have to do that," I told him afterward, a little embarrassed that he might have bid so high to impress me.

"Oh, I know," he said quietly. "But I thought it would be fun for your kids if we took them to New York." It was only our fourth date!

That's when I really started to fall for him. Not only was he genuine, considerate, and generous, he was also factoring in my children. By that stage of my life, I had begun to doubt that I would ever meet a man who was prepared to embrace the whole package that I had to offer: my children, my past, and my career. That night made me think that Barry might actually be interested in all those facets of my life. But what really sealed the deal for me was when Jackson refused to give him a nickname—just totally declined the opportunity. I was floored. Barry—whom I had dutifully prepared for what I thought would be his inevitable dubious christening—was actually disappointed, but I assured him, "*Trrrust* me. You don't want a nickname."

Barry frequently had business in New York, so he met the three of us there on our trip. He took Jackson, who was twelve, to the floor of the stock exchange, and we all went to the opera and to see the Rockettes, which was the perfect New York experience for Stephanie, whose six-year-old attention span was held by the glitz of the performance. It was a great trip, and he was good with the kids. They really started to bond with him. After we returned home, our relationship quickly evolved.

We'd been dating for about six months when we went on a couples weekend getaway in the Pacific Northwest with my girlfriend Barbara and her husband. We had just watched the inauguration of George W. Bush, and the two of us were talking. I was happy. I looked at him and said, "So. Where is this going?"

"Well . . . I think it's going along just fine. Why?"

"I'm not fine with it kind of going along just fine forever."

"What do you mean?"

"I mean we're either moving in the direction of marriage, or we're not. I love you, and I'd like to know which it is." For the second time, I was laying my heart out there.

"Oh . . . all right," he said. "Well, I'll think about that."

I hate wasting time. I knew, with Barry, I would have to nudge him if I expected our relationship to progress. I loved him and wanted to be with him, but I wasn't interested in staying involved if he didn't want to share his life with my children and me.

Luckily, he did.

There were no annulments to wait for this time, and we decided to put a wedding together in three months. I was still working unforgiving hours in the State Senate, so my girlfriends took over and essentially became my wedding planners; they were an exuberant committee. The matchmaker, Kathleen, hosted the engagement party. My friend Deborah planned a great beach event the night before the wedding. Jessica McClintock, another Merry Widow at the time, made my dress—a beautiful burgundy gown. Stephanie and all of my friends' daughters were my flower girls. With everybody's help, it all fell into place, and on a gorgeous day in 2001, Barry and I got married at the mission in Carmel, with Father Dan presiding over the ceremony. And Helen, another fellow Merry, hosted the wedding reception at her beautiful home over the cliffs of the Pacific Ocean. Since we were married at the Carmel mission, I decided on a Hispanic theme; we even had a mariachi band. It was a beautiful celebration. The unimaginable had happened: I was truly happy again.

There has never been any superficiality or posturing with Barry. His straightforward nature is one of the qualities I continue to cherish. And, much to my surprise, one of the extraordinary elements that he brought to my life has been a real appreciation of the Midwest and of traditional midwestern values. We have a log cabin in Michigan, where Barry goes fly-fishing, and we all go boating and walking in the woods, taking in the simpler pleasures of nature that I never would have predicted could bring me such delight. He brought his brother-in-law and sister, Bruce and Mary Pons, into my life, and over the weeks we've spent together, both in the cabin and at their home in Palm Springs, she's become the sister I never had. But the cabin is where we recharge our batteries, where family and friends come to enjoy the lake, and where life is pure.

But incorporating Barry's values, and our marriage overall, into our lives was an adjustment for my family. Jackson and Barry got along immediately, but it took Stephanie more time to warm up. She had never known her own father and never had to share me with an adult. Barry, reliable and steady, stuck with it and really worked to earn Stephanie's trust.

Naturally, there were challenges for Barry, too. Having been on his own for his whole life meant that he had fostered an independent sensibility. That's proven helpful in our lives together, given the amount of time I spend away from home, but it initially demanded a real adjustment for him. By now, he has gotten used to my chaotic lifestyle. He not only was willing to embrace everything about me, he also wanted to adopt Jackson and Stephanie. He waited until we thought Stephanie was ready, which took five years into the marriage. He then proposed the idea to the kids on the dock at the lake by the cabin. They both accepted. I continue to feel so blessed that he came into my life, secure in my faith that he was part of the plan for me. That has only become more true as we've continued our days together.

The year after Barry and I got married, I was elected to my second term as a state senator in a comfortable race. That time around, my constituents knew me well enough to vote me in by about 78 percent. The gift of having Barry as a husband freed me up to relish my time with my children without always worrying about the inevitable details of running our home as a single mom. Without those extra worries, I focused a sharper eye on my career, and on the issues that affected Californians.

Easing the plight of women who deserve more than they're receiving has always been at the forefront of my agenda. One of the toughest-fought battles in my career was waged over child support. When I was on the County Board of Supervisors, we held a hearing that we called the *Feminization of Poverty*. We had noticed a trend of single mothers who were falling below the poverty line, largely because their court-ordered child support simply wasn't being paid by the other parent and California's enforcement on the issue was weak. When I got to the state legislature, my staff and I drafted bills that made it so anyone who held a professional state license of any kind (medical, driver's, whatever) and was also in arrears with child support payments was subject to losing their license if they didn't develop a viable plan for repayment. When we were passing that bill, my kids were very young. I was working long hours trying to gain support for the initiative when my office received a death threat. I can't imagine it was the only one, but the police and my staff found it credible enough to issue me body armor that I wore every day, along with twenty-four-hour protection. They moved Jackson, Stephanie, and me to a hotel for a few days while they investigated the threat. Tensions were high, and there were quite a few constituents who knew they stood to receive one of the hundreds of thousands of notices that would be sent out in the first few years.

The first person who got nailed on a professional license was a doctor in San Diego who owed over $100,000 in back payments. He hadn't bothered to support his children's upbringing until his own livelihood was threatened. Then he cared. In the first decade of the bill, the DMV sent out 403,000 notices to drivers saying that they were going to lose their license. Half of those drivers paid what they owed immediately, approximately 144,000 paid eventually, and roughly 66,000 lost their licenses. Primary caregivers collected over $400 million in delinquent court-ordered payments, helping thousands of mothers and families escape poverty.

That was when our office really hummed, when we were successfully conjuring up ways to amend the law to benefit those who actually needed help. One of the last bills we passed to remedy that problem was to make the Franchise Tax Board the collector of last resort—so if someone wasn't paying their child support, but had a refund on their tax return, the state would take it and use it to pay the custodial parent.

All in all, over $800 million of court-ordered child support was returned to custodial parents. The bills weren't crafted or passed with ease, but I had a resilient staff who never gave up on an issue. I can't say that all of our endeavors yielded the precise changes we were seeking, but we got a lot accomplished, which was immensely satisfying.

During my second and final term in the State Senate, I deliberated about whether I should take a shot at running for lieutenant governor of California. I knew it would be a tough race: the other candidates were an insurance commissioner and another female state senator, who would draw key votes from me. I knew that the race was tough—possibly unwinnable—but I was certain that I wanted to stay involved in public service, and fear of failure hadn't been an excuse for me before. Abraham Lincoln failed in business and lost eight major elections before he became president. Babe Ruth led the American league in home runs for twelve seasons, but also led the league in strikeouts for five seasons. J. K. Rowling's first Harry Potter book was rejected by over a dozen publishers and she was told to keep her day job. That familiar adage stared at me from a paperweight on my desk: *What would you attempt to do if you knew you could not fail?* The debate didn't last for too long in my mind. *Of course I have to run,* I decided.

There was (what felt like) a great deal of interest in seeing me continue in government, and my team knew how to run a campaign, which made it feel manageable. The race was long, over two years, and it was a pressure cooker, with ups and downs and me driving all over the state and selling myself day in and day out. I put out two commercials, statewide, and finished one of them by looking at the camera and saying, "If you want to know what I'll do, look at what I've done." I was proud of everything our team had accomplished in the assembly and Senate, and wanted California to know that I was eager to stand on my record and be accountable.

The ensuing polls gave us reason to hope we might eke our way through to another victory. It was forecasted that I would win by 1 to 3 percent, so I knew it was going to be close, no matter what. But I had been in close races before, and I allowed myself to remain optimistic. In the end, the insurance commissioner won, by less than 3 percent of the vote. It stung—my loyal core had put so much into the race, and we had led the candidates in campaign funds and received statewide newspaper endorsements. It was a depressing moment for the team. I was more crushed than I would have thought; I felt like I had let down all of the exceptional people who had been so steadfast in their support of me over the years.

The morning after I lost, I woke up feeling drugged. It was as though I had almost summited a mountain, only to have stumbled down. The morning after my loss was also Jackson's high school graduation, and I wanted my focus to be exclusively on him. I was overjoyed: it was his day to shine, but at the same time, I had no desire to face all those parents who knew I had just lost the primary. I had no desire to hear or respond to the inevitable "I really thought you had it in the bag" conversations.

As I dressed and prepared for the day ahead, I heard my father's words resounding in my mind: "Get over it, Jackie." This time that unsympathetic sentiment inspired me—it reminded me of a far tougher time. I licked my wounds for a few minutes, dusted myself off, and got ready to celebrate our son. After the ceremony Barry and I had a party for him in our backyard. As I watched him laughing with his friends, I was beaming, reminded that there is really nothing more rewarding and important than witnessing your children's happiness and success.

After the excitement over Jackson's graduation waned, however, I was physically and emotionally exhausted. My campaign finance director extraordinaire, Christine Krolik, was my closest friend through the process and had witnessed the race from beginning to end. She knew how drained I was feeling. A few mornings later I got a call from her. "Jackie, we've got to start doing yoga." *Well, why not*, I thought. I wasn't sure where I was headed next, and it seemed like a revitalizing choice for my body and spirit.

Christine introduced me to Margo Kramer, a seventy-two-year-old yoga instructor who did headstands and splits with the agility and grace of a twenty-year-old ballerina. I was sold. We put together a group of friends who would come to my house every Friday for class. We were all novices, but also all devoted to bettering ourselves and having fun. And like many times before in my life, a new family of strong women was formed. The yoga group started with devoting that one day of the week to sprawling our mats, blocks, and blankets out on my living room floor and going through the positions. Over time, our sisterhood developed into another great reason to take girlfriend trips to Puerto Vallarta or Palm Springs. Sometimes there is yoga, but—not unlike the Merry Widows—our time together is primarily defined by the resounding, comforting laughter we share.

I needed those treasured distractions during that moment, not only because of the political loss and career uncertainty, but because the situation in our home had become a less-than-serene portrait of the sandwich generation. Not long after we married, Barry's father passed away, and his mom, Betty, came from Wisconsin to live with us. Soon after, as my mother was becoming less self-sufficient, she also moved in, which meant Barry and I both had our moms at home with our family. Betty was a genuinely lovely woman and lived with us for five years. As she grew older, she lost almost all her eyesight, and toward the end of her time with us, she was virtually blind. Meanwhile, Mom was practically deaf by the time she moved into our home. So we had the two mothers—one who couldn't see, the other who couldn't hear, and neither one was crazy about the other. The whole thing could have been a sitcom, with Barry and me tripping over walkers and oxygen tanks.

My father had already moved into assisted living. They had been married for nearly sixty years, but Mom decided not to move in with him, as she had zero interest in communal living. She kept their house in Belmont, visited Dad a couple of days a week, continued to work, and lived alone until she moved in with us. She was much too independent to feel comfortable in a group environment, but my father absolutely loved it. He was a handsome and distinguished man throughout his life, and he really held court in that place. The women would gather round as he regaled them with colorful stories of his life (many of which were likely fabricated). He never lost the sharpness of his mind, let alone the characteristic sparkle in his blue eyes.

Chapter Nine

CAPITOL HILL

For a very brief moment, I thought I was done with politics. I had made a good run of it, but it was time to focus my attention elsewhere. At the same time, I knew from the first morning I woke up without work that my purpose had not been fulfilled yet. I wanted to continue to be relevant. I wanted to change people's lives for the better, for as long as I could. So I quickly took a job with a San Francisco law firm, determined that I could find a way to carry on my public service in the private sector. But I missed politics. When I found out that Congressman Tom Lantos, a fourteen-term incumbent, was vacating his congressional seat—the seat that had originally been held by Leo Ryan—I was itching for an excuse to return. The district was stunned by Lantos's announcement. I couldn't ignore the way my gut lurched when I heard the news. After my first failed attempt following Guyana, I had thought I would never run for Congress again. But if I had absorbed anything, it was that—just as in life or love—I had to expect the unexpected.

Nobody taps you on the shoulder and tells you to run for office—you have to feel it, take the plunge, and be prepared for failure. I was ready for that, if my family was. Barry was supportive, and Jackson was already in college, so he was removed from the chaos that a campaign and potential congressional seat would bring; but Stephanie was still in high school. Before I filed the papers, we discussed whether she felt she could manage with my being gone a few days a week. She knew it was what I wanted, but I also wanted her to understand that a big part of my motivation was to help make the country a better place for her and Jackson, and this congressional race felt like the best route to making real change. She looked at me like I was a little crazy for asking and said that she'd be fine—she wanted me to go for it.

Each of my losses had prepared me well over my career. Had I not run for Congress and lost, I wouldn't have been ready to run for supervisor. This time around, had I not run for lieutenant governor and lost, I wouldn't have had the same overwhelming support for my second attempt at a congressional seat. In January 2008, I announced that I was going to run in the Democratic primary. Other potential candidates did some polling, saw that I had a sizable lead, and decided not to run. The following month, amid the flurry of the beginning of a race, Congressman Lantos unexpectedly died of cancer. It was a sad moment that suddenly accelerated everything, and on April 8, 2008, I won the election to serve out the remaining months of his term. A whirlwind three months after announcing my candidacy, I was heading to the floor of Congress to be sworn in by Nancy Pelosi, the first female Speaker of the House of Representatives and a longtime political friend and colleague. (In June, I ran again to serve a full term in Congress and secured 85 percent of the vote to remain in the same seat that Ryan had once held.) As I prepared to set up my partial life on the other side of the country, I steeled my determination to carry my late mentor's integrity and pragmatism back to Washington. I was finally going to take my seat in the halls of Congress. It had only taken me twenty-nine years to get there.

I braced myself for Congress, bolstered by the slightly naive confidence that my experience getting things done in California had prepared me for negotiating similar deals on a national scale. It didn't take long until I was disabused of the notion that common sense was going to be greatly applicable to business as usual in our Capitol. Nothing could have prepared me for the egregious curveballs and dysfunction that awaited me in Washington.

I've wondered how I might have managed the job had I somehow won my first run for Congressman Ryan's seat, in 1979. I would have shown up in Washington, DC, not yet thirty years old, serving under President Jimmy Carter, physically hindered and emotionally raw. I'm sure I would have caught up and adjusted to the pace and the mores of the town, but it would have been a very steep climb, and I'm not sure I would have been as resilient as I was when I arrived with nearly three decades of elected office under my belt. By 2008 I was well versed in how best to represent my constituents, I understood California's issues in all their complexities, and I was fired up to address them on a national stage—perhaps a little too confident and hopeful that all the hours of hard work I'd applied to forging compromises with adversaries in Sacramento would offer me a road map to achieving similar successes in Washington. In moments of acute optimism, I imagined myself striking common ground between the parties.

Though determined to start building bridges as soon as I got there, I hadn't expected everything to move quite so quickly. The weeks leading up to my swearing-in ceremony were a surreal tornado as I prepared for my new role and its responsibilities. We had a big celebratory pancake breakfast to say thank you and goodbye to all of the constituents who had stuck by me through the years. I was presented with a brand-new, undented suitcase by the yoga girls, and with it I boarded the plane for Washington to be sworn in to Congress. It was a high moment of joy—there were about two dozen family members and supporters who flew out from the Bay Area to help commemorate my entering Congress.

That swearing-in, however, ended up being a stark reminder that I was going to have to learn to play by a whole different set of rules.

My first day in the United States House of Representatives, my family and new staff members watched from the gallery as Speaker Pelosi administered the oath of office. Most members of Congress are elected in November and sworn in as a group on the first day of the session in January. If someone is elected in a special midterm election, he or she is sworn in individually, and the new member is offered the opportunity to take a few minutes to address the House. All I knew was that I would have three minutes to give my first speech on that hallowed floor. No one told me there were rules, expectations, or precedents to follow regarding what is said or not said in such remarks.

Congressman Pete Stark, the dean of the California delegation and an old friend of Leo Ryan's, introduced me. He and Congressman Ryan had served together. A California Republican congressman, Jerry Lewis, then stood up and welcomed me. I'm sure he never imagined, when he came and saw me, immobile in Arlington, that three decades later he'd be congratulating me as a colleague. I certainly couldn't have predicted such a leap. So it was very moving to come full circle with him; hearing him announce my name to the House filled me with pride. My dear friends and members of Congress Anna Eshoo and Mike Thompson (who had been my chief of staff in the state assembly) stood beside me and were flanked by the other California members from both parties. After Congressman Stark's kind welcome, I approached the podium and began my three minutes. I thanked Speaker Pelosi and praised the legacy of Congressman Tom Lantos, a champion for human rights and the only Holocaust survivor to serve in Congress. I thanked everybody who had supported me and spent a moment honoring Congressman Ryan, all of which was warmly received.

Everything was running smoothly, until I launched into my political concern. The biggest issue from my campaign had been my conviction to help end the war in Iraq. My constituents were in rare agreement that entering the war had been a devastating mistake; they felt the country had been lied to about weapons of mass destruction and were fed up with President Bush's foreign policy. I told my new colleagues that my constituents were demanding an end to the war and began to quickly unpack my feelings on the travesty of the conflict.

Midspeech, I heard someone boo. It struck me as rude, but I carried on: "The process to bring the troops home must begin immediately. The president wants to stay the course, and a man who wants to replace him [Arizona Senator John McCain, then running for president] suggests we could be in Iraq for a hundred years." The booing gained decided volume. I looked out and identified who was leading the jeers; it was Darrell Issa, a Republican from Southern California who was the richest man in Congress at the time and presently remains a staunch supporter of Donald Trump. Issa wasn't just booing; he was leading a short parade of Republicans out of the chamber, beckoning others to join his walkout. My new Democratic colleagues saw the dissent and came to my defense, applauding to drown out the boos. Unnerved by the unexpected snub but emboldened by the counter of support, I finished, "Madam Speaker, history will not judge us kindly if we sacrifice four generations of Americans because of the folly of one."

Later, a *Politico* reporter clued me in to the fact that remarks made after being sworn in are supposed to steer clear of politics. I wasn't upset so much as sheepish: I had been a congresswoman for less than five minutes and had already run afoul of the institution. The only time in recent history that someone had been booed at a swearing-in was in 1987, the reporter said, when Nancy Pelosi herself dared to castigate Congress for doing nothing to combat AIDS, the dominant issue in her district at the time. I caught sight of her smiling face coming to congratulate me and instantly felt better about my faux pas—at least I was in good company. Ever since the swearing-in, any disregard of institutional practices on my part has been deliberate.

I arrived in Congress at an especially challenging time for the country. By October 2008, the global economy was on the brink of collapse. I assembled a close team of experts, and we held several town halls in San Francisco to discuss the tanking economy and what we were going to do about it. I voted for the government bailout, as I knew I should, but found it agonizing, a devastating demonstration of Wall Street's outsized influence over policy in our nation. As I was still new to Congress, however, I maintained some hope that the immense challenge of putting our economy back together might galvanize the parties to cease squabbling and instead forge alliances to limit the damage done by that once-in-a-generation financial crisis. That hope was kept alight when, a month later, the country elected Barack Obama as our 44th president. Though I had been a Hillary supporter in the primary, the national swell of excitement surrounding Obama's election was electrifying, and seemed to portend all sorts of fresh possibilities for our politics and discourse. It wouldn't take long, however, to witness what the president-elect was up against.

My personal transition to Washington was not as seamless as I might have hoped, either. One of the most challenging revelations was Stephanie's dissatisfaction with the new realities that Congress brought to our lives. She was less than thrilled about how much time I was spending away from home, though I tried my best to keep to a routine: four nights a week at home and three in Washington. It's rough being an adolescent girl, period. But it's especially hard when you have parents whose jobs pull them away from you. Her discontent, coupled with the demands my new role imposed, made for an exhausting shift. Stephanie and Barry went to counseling, learned to communicate a little better, and grew to understand each other. In time, I figured out how to manage my schedule and energy so that when I was home, I could actually be present and available. I devote the weekends to Barry and the kids, then we always have a special Sunday dinner, which I love. It has been a real ritual for us, and includes decorating the dining table, a tradition inherited from Aunt Tobie that I've always adored. We invite our friends over—including familiar regulars from ACSS, the Merry Widows, or the yoga girls—and Barry cooks a spectacular dinner. Engaging the requisite endurance and tenacity for daily battles in Washington would not be sustainable if I didn't make time to nourish my home life in this way. Those simple Sunday-night dinners were and are my favorite escape from the pressures of work, and a reliable opportunity to make sure I am staying connected with my dearest ones.

My parents were still alive when I took office in Washington, and it was also hard to spend less time with them, especially when my mom moved in. She was never shy about her commentary regarding the kind of mother I was being for Stephanie. Dad was very proud of my political endeavors, and kept everybody at the assisted-living home more informed on my work accomplishments than any of them needed to be. And though my mother would see me on TV and say, "You look tired; are you not getting enough sleep?" she would apparently then go and boast about me to the upholstery classes she was still teaching. Whenever I was home and there was an event that I could convince her to attend, I would dress Mom for it with some of my clothes—we were roughly the same size. Since she had sewed all of my clothes for the first two decades of my life, rendering a serviceable wardrobe, I spent my adolescence without anything that could ever be identified as being particularly stylish. (There was one notable exception: a beautiful dress that I adored, with whole and sliced lemons on a white background. The fabric was so memorable that when Kate Spade put out a line featuring lemons a few years ago, I splurged on an exorbitantly priced top for no reason other than that the fabric reminded me of my mom.) Mom wouldn't allow me to dress her in anything too fashionable, but she did agree to wear a bright-pink suit of mine for her ninetieth birthday party. She looked truly beautiful. Then in 2009, we hosted a big retirement party for her. It was around Mardi Gras, so that was the theme, and all of her students came for a colorful celebration. It was a party of respect and revelry, honoring her forty years at the school.

Less than three weeks after Mom stopped working, she started on hospice, though she wasn't aware of it. She had congestive heart failure, but the doctors had told us she had another six months to live—perhaps they were optimistic because of the unyielding spirit that she exuded. On a Thursday, I had taken the late flight home from Washington. It was around eight o'clock by the time I unlocked the door. Later, when I was putting her to bed, I suggested that she drink a little Ensure, because she wasn't eating enough.

"Now?" she said, aghast. "I can't eat this *now*! And why are you coming home so *late*?" I believe those were her last words to me. I eventually convinced her to drink a little and settled her into bed. When I woke up at three in the morning and went to check on her, I found her frothing at the mouth. Panicked, I hurried to call the night nurse, who gently informed me that my mom was passing. I hung up the phone and slowly made my way to her bedside, where I held her small, tough hand and listening to her labored breathing. An hour later I woke up Stephanie, and the two of us sat with Mom. I whispered into her ear that I loved her and that we were there by her side. I hope that helped her go peacefully, knowing that she wasn't alone. It was a humbling, even in some ways beautiful, opportunity for our three generations of women to be together as Mom took her last breath. The nurse called minutes after she passed and wanted to immediately call the mortuary. "No," I said firmly. "We'll call them later." I wanted Dad to have the opportunity to say goodbye. First thing, I drove over to the home and brought him back to be with her. He sat beside Mom and sweetly, quietly, cried.

I knew that the best way to honor her legacy was to keep on working, to never stop getting things done. After Mom's funeral, I settled back into my routine of spending three or four days of the week in

Washington. When I was there, I strove to be fiercely productive. But the rancor and procedural gridlock I faced in the halls of Congress continued to shock and disappoint me. Hard work in Sacramento had yielded dividends for me that clearly progressed our state forward. I had presumed that the national system would work in a similar fashion. I was wrong.

The generally civil tenor of Sacramento was a world apart from daily affairs in Washington, a reality that set in with the force of whiplash. Every role model in my life, as far back as the Sisters at Mercy, had instilled in me the necessity to act; unfortunately, I learned that Congress often feeds on *not* acting. That's especially true of the current administration, in which members are expected to serve as robotic voting machines, always toeing the party line. The supposed powers that be do not like ingenuity, and they do not like independence. Not to mention the importance placed on seniority. Newly elected members can't get much done unless they convince someone who's been there much longer to get on board. Committees are generally run by the most senior member; longevity is valued over integrity; and new ideas are often dismissed exclusively on the grounds of being new ideas. There are hundreds of brilliant representatives and staffers who work tirelessly to help the country evolve. But there are customs and there are barriers in Washington—everywhere.

In Washington's arena, reels of red tape and red ties regularly obstruct forward motion. After a decade playing on the national stage, I've learned to adjust my expectations while doing my best to keep from backing down or being silent. Barriers can be broken if you're smart about it, and even when you're working in a body of 435 sanctioned individuals, amid deafening, shallow rhetoric, you can still find common ground. But it took me time to learn how to navigate the strange waters of our government.

Even after all this time, and with increasing regularity, it seems that every week there's another incident that causes me to look at some of my colleagues and genuinely wonder, *Who* are *these people?* That invariably leads me to: *Who am* I? *Am I nuts? Do I get pleasure from hitting my head against the Capitol's marble and granite walls?* Truth be told, I don't, but I cannot deny that I love a good fight, and have maintained a propulsive passion for slaying dragons. And there are plenty in our midst.

After Mom died in 2009, the foundation of my life back home shifted in a number of ways. Betty, my mother-in-law who had been with us for five years, died three months later. In 2010 I turned sixty, which felt like more of a landmark moment than I had anticipated. I spent the day with the yoga girls—by chance, another one was receiving a Citizen of the Year award in Half Moon Bay, and I was asked to introduce her at an event that night. When I entered the venue, a man asked me to get on a horse. "Um . . . no, thank you," I said, looking around in confusion. The guy turned to me and sighed. "Lady, you'd be doing me a big favor if you'd just get on this horse." His entreaty, combined with the sounds of a mariachi band, tipped me off to what was going on. So I got on the horse and was ridden down a small hill. At the bottom, a hundred people jumped out and hollered, *"Surprise!"* It was such a moving evening—especially when Stephanie led the yoga girls in a choreographed dance and song about me, followed by an unforgettable dance with my dad, who was in a wheelchair at the time but still reveled in the celebration. A few months later, my sweet Jackson graduated from Stanford. I was so proud of him and excited that he was entering the world, but also felt incredibly emotional about letting him go.

I felt similarly thrilled and emotional when Stephanie graduated from Mercy in 2012. She sang at the baccalaureate Mass, which was stunning. Dad was still there in his wheelchair, beaming up at his Mickey Mouse, all grown up. Stephanie went off to college, and we returned home to the sad news that a bone scan had revealed that Dad had cancer all over his body. I decided I wouldn't let him die in a hospital. So we bought a hospital bed and moved him back to our house. We called Stephanie and suggested she come back that weekend. She arrived on Friday, and though Dad had been given several months to live, he died the following Monday. It was Labor Day, which felt very apt, given the ethos that had brought him and Mom together. They had worked so hard throughout their entire lives, being sure to leave their children with better odds than those that they had been dealt.

My family will always be my priority, so with all the landmark changes going on at home, my voting record went through a bit of a dry spell. Even so, I was finding my footing in Congress, and began leading initiatives on the causes to which I felt particularly devoted. I started working in earnest to help alleviate the confounding crisis of sexual assault in the military. It's an essential, revered institution, but also one resistant to rethinking its traditions. I spoke with everyone from the secretary of defense to four-star generals to countless servicemembers. Each year, twenty thousand of those servicemembers are sexually assaulted. From those, roughly five thousand report the crime, but because of our twisted system, only five hundred of those go to court-martial, and only two hundred fifty get convictions, after the grueling, alienating process. With those kinds of odds, why would anybody report? It remains this dirty secret that our government refuses to confront properly, which is why most of the women and men to whom I've spoken acknowledged that they feel the double punch of victimization: first by their attacker, then by the institution that prevented them from seeking justice. We introduced legislation to hold perpetrators responsible, and have made very small gains in terms of shedding light on an endemic institutional failure. We're still working on it; and I'm still having those conversations. As a reminder of the courage and heroism of all the victims who have come to my office and stood up to report the crimes committed against them, I keep a military helmet on my office bureau signed by servicemembers who have survived sexual assault. Looking at it keeps their voices ringing in my ears and inspires me to keep fighting for them.

Working on such issues and meeting so many roadblocks in Washington highlighted just how essential it was for me to find like-minded fighters among my colleagues. Thankfully, I have by no means felt alone in the daily battle to make good trouble in our government. After a decade here, I have identified plenty of admirable allies.

Toward the end of my latest term, on June 12, 2016, the massacre of forty-nine people in Orlando—the worst mass shooting in our history at the time (it has since been eclipsed by the Las Vegas shooting of October 1, 2017)—occurred. It hit an especially raw nerve to see the footage from the nightclub. I recognized all too well the confusion, fear, and devastation on the faces of the victims. Later that month, Georgia Congressman John Lewis, the heroic veteran of creative disruption, led one hundred seventy members of Congress in a protest on the floor of the House of Representatives. The sit-in lasted for twenty-five hours, an extraordinary showing of government leaders who demanded a vote on measures to expand background checks and block gun purchases by suspected terrorists.

I was in California at the time, sitting at UCSF Medical Center, watching my colleagues make history on TV as my brother, Eric, was undergoing surgery. Eric had joined the Coast Guard and then the postal service, and has made a great life for himself. He inherited my parents' industrious genes. In his free time, he goes around to garage sales to buy things, then fixes them up and sells them for five times as much.

Like all hospital vigils, waiting through Eric's surgery was anxious and consuming, but the moment I heard that his operation had been successful and saw him back in his hospital room doing well, I knew I needed to be in Washington. I didn't have much time to catch the ten o'clock flight, but I couldn't head to the airport without running home to retrieve a relic from a long-unopened drawer, an item I had only once before taken out in public. I grabbed the small plastic sleeve and hurried to SFO. After what felt like an interminable flight, I arrived on the floor of the House, several hours after Republican leadership had shut off the lights in an attempt to silence the sitting Democrats. I stepped up to the podium in front of my brave and persistent colleagues. In my hand I held the little plastic sleeve, at the top of which was written, *EVIDENCE. FEDERAL BUREAU OF INVESTIGATION*. Inside the sleeve was a dumdum, a particularly nasty bullet designed to maximize human destruction once it's been shot. The bullet had been removed from beneath my armpit, a year after my return from Jonestown. After surgery, the FBI took the bullet, did ballistics tests on it, and returned it to me in that little plastic sleeve with evidence tape wrapped around it. It had always struck me as a gruesome, unnecessary souvenir, until we conducted that sit-in, where my evidence served a renewed purpose. The bullet that was supposed to kill me underscored our message: we cannot continue with business as usual in this country.

The majority was doing its best to shut out the public, and ordered that the news cameras be shut down. So we turned to social media to transmit images and video of our protest—using Facebook, Twitter, and Periscope to let in the American public. C-SPAN picked up a stream on Periscope from a fellow California representative's phone. Though no legislation followed that sit-in, there was a triumphant silver lining to the experience: we learned that there is always a way to make your message heard.

Politics are divisive and don't always bring out the best in us. Silencing colleagues, refusing to vote on issues—those tactics slow the progress of our country. It's no secret that progressing through these troubling times can be confounding. But it's not impossible. The struggle continues up a very steep hill in the gun-violence prevention battle, because guns are such a deeply ingrained part of our culture. Add special interests and the greed of those who sell guns without bothering to do a background check, and you get capable legislators—whose job it is to vote on and write legislation—actively refusing to bring forward bills that could close loopholes on who can buy a gun, and where. Sensible amendments that could help prevent the deaths of more than thirty-three thousand Americans each year (with almost three times as many injured). Instead, the government's responses to mass shootings have been dozens of moments of silence, followed by legislative silence.

The world's most powerful deliberative body regularly uses our collective might to do nothing. Ever since the San Bernardino attack's moment of silence, I've walked off the floor or not been present. Hollow statements always set off my outrage meter. I'm not going to stand up for one more of these moments, knowing that nothing of substance will follow, so I've continued to boycott the chamber, or walk out when these posturing pauses occur. They're an intolerable show of hypocrisy, and speak to our impotence that we think that it's good enough to take out a minute to pray, then get back to our business. The families of murdered loved ones deserve more than an acknowledgment—they deserve action. And there is no reason why we have allowed our society to be so overridden by guns. It's one thing to support the Second Amendment; it's another thing to embrace weapons of war. They are instruments of lethal power.

Bullets maim. They demolish. The notion that there can be a "full recovery" after a bullet has entered your body belies reality. We don't spend enough time thinking about the people who survive gunshot wounds. It is a long and oftentimes incomplete road back to a functional existence. Other members of Congress have been shot while I was in office: Gabby Giffords and Steve Scalise. They are irrevocably damaged, emotionally and physically. Gabby's survival is nothing less than a miracle. She has true grit, but her life has been transformed, and it is not easy. Steve Scalise, who was shot at a baseball practice with fellow members of Congress, now moves around in a scooter or on crutches. He's endured numerous surgeries and may well have more in the future.

I no longer feel ambushed with each retelling of my own experience of getting shot. My body functions as well as it possibly can. But a car backfiring or a violent scene in a movie still reverberates through me. Fireworks continue to make me tremble. Twenty-one-gun salutes terrify me. Because even when a bullet doesn't kill, it annihilates in ways that—without the experience of being shot—are difficult to understand. A gunshot wound is a theft. It takes something that you will never get back, whether it's your hearing, your leg, or the ability to feel comfortable in a crowd of people. The lucky among us may keep breathing, we may keep active, and we may have gained a perspective that helps us live our life more fully. But make no mistake—we are maimed for life. Bullets destroy. It is their purpose. And what they take from our flesh and our soul can never be recovered.

I have two bullets inside of my body; I am in a powerful position where I could do something about the type of violence and weapons that put them there, and yet nothing has changed. I'm ashamed of that. It's horrifying how often our great flag flies at half mast. It infuriates me that the NRA has infiltrated our government to such an extent that a sane conversation can't be had about this crisis. There has been one mass shooting after another in our beautiful country. The reason why seventeen teenagers died in Parkland, Florida, the reason why their parents were screaming and crying on TV as they searched for their children, was because their assailant had access to an assault weapon and was able to discharge as many bullets as he did. The fresh, young voices of the survivors of that attack have ignited a revolution, and they tuned in very quickly to the first necessary step: reinstate the assault-weapon ban. Weapons of war have no place in the hands of a civilian. Sweeping these attacks to the side by labeling them mental health issues, or blaming video games, is a mistake that turns a blind eye to the most important part of the conversation. No kid needs an assault weapon. No adult needs an assault weapon. We have miles to go beyond that, but my years in Washington have taught me that progress is gained in small steps forward.

When I took office, I never would have imagined that the numbers would escalate until more children were killed by gun violence in the US each year than were servicemembers in Iraq and Afghanistan combined. Hundreds of thousands of innocent Americans, from nightclubgoers, to church attendants, to schoolchildren, have been shot while I was in office. And we have done nothing about it. I can only hope, and keep fighting, and maintain the conviction of the perhaps out-of-order woman I was when I stood at the podium in 2008 and spoke my mind, determined to amend Washington's status quo.

Chapter Ten

SHATTERING SILENCE

Expecting the unexpected got catapulted to a whole new level in January 2017, when Donald Trump was sworn in as president of the United States. The morning after the inauguration, I hosted a breakfast reception at the Capitol, mobilizing hundreds of women—many of whom were from my congressional district—in the fight to ratify the Equal Rights Amendment (ERA) and to make women's rights a priority in the 115th Congress. That proposed amendment, twenty-four simple words that would make it illegal to discriminate against citizens based on sex, has been proposed in Congress without adoption since 1923. Most people are shocked to learn that sad truth about our Constitution. In an interview given by Supreme Court Justice Antonin Scalia in 2011, he provoked outrage by stating, "Certainly the Constitution does not require discrimination on the basis of sex. The only issue is whether it prohibits it. It doesn't." He was correct. And the inauguration seemed a perfect day to send a message to the Republicans ruling Congress, to the incoming administration, and to the American people that women were not going to be treated as second-class citizens. We were not going to allow over a century's worth of hard-won rights to be rolled back even an inch.

To me, to many of my colleagues, and to much of the nation, we sent that response in 2017. It was a critical year to come together and aggressively address discrimination in all of its corrosive and violent forms. It was the tipping point when enough outraged women stood up, fed up and determined to take matters into our own hands. There was no more exhilarating affirmation of this than the Women's March that took place in cities across the world, and was among the most heartening political uprisings I'd ever witnessed.

I have been in politics for most of my life, and have seen a remarkable change in the conversation. When I was a Ryan Girl and for years after, *feminism* was practically a dirty word. I have been fighting for laws to protect women for my entire adult life. Sometimes I have had to settle for incremental reforms, rationalizing that half a loaf was better than no loaf at all. Other times I stuck my high heels in the sand and drew a line, and often I was forced to wait for a more optimal time to act. In 2014, I tried to pass an amendment to mandate sexual-harassment-prevention training in Congress. The chairman of the Rules Committee did not even allow the measure to be debated. I tried to add more funding for the compliance office to do proper outreach, but that money was removed. I was battling for improvements, but there was no willingness to listen. At times I left those sessions feeling so deflated. But giving up was never an option or a consideration.

Though I've fought for causes ranging from environmental protection to privacy laws, there are a few that I'm never tired of championing, marquee issues that I've prioritized since my first pamphlet as a San Mateo County Supervisor candidate. Chief among them is women's empowerment. A campaign consultant once advised me, with the best of intentions, to not be *so* focused on women, that doing so would only alienate men. But I responded, and still believe, "If women don't do it, who will?" If a woman avoids taking on the cause of women, who do we expect to affect change? Should we leave it to men to fight for our equal pay? I know that, as a woman, I am a minority in the House—in the most diverse Congress ever elected, we still only make up 20 percent of the representatives, yet we are more than half the population of the United States. In fact, I was only the 217th woman of over twelve thousand members to serve in the House of Representatives. In the history of our country to date, only 289 women have served, but that is about to change. It is no surprise that I feel a huge responsibility to fight for laws that protect and equalize women and their daughters and granddaughters. So I've always been at my most dogged when it comes to issues like domestic violence and sexual assault within our military, on college campuses, in the workplace, and on the Hill.

The abuse of power, especially toward women, has always felt deeply personal. I know that I am far from alone in having experienced sexual abuse. I dealt with that horror as a child, and the memory of feeling so vulnerable, confused, and disgraced has shaped me irrevocably. As is too often the case, I was abused by a family member; in my case it was my grandfather. It's astonishing how many children are sexually abused in their homes. Often it's the uncle, the stepparent, the cousin. It's more prevalent than will ever come to the surface, I fear. My own recollection is fuzzy, because I was quite young, and long ago willed it out of my memories. What I do remember is that I would stay with my grandparents when I was six or seven and take naps with my grandfather in the bedroom. They had German duvets, so it was nice and cozy under those goose-feather covers. He would fondle me and put his hand inside of me. Sometimes he would place my leg against his penis. I knew what was happening was not right, but I had no idea what to do about it. So I did nothing. I don't remember how many times it happened. Probably five or six, though I can't say for certain. I also don't know precisely when, or how, but the behavior stopped.

There is a human instinct to suppress such horrors and violations, and that's what I did for years, burying what had been done to me under a layer of shame. But it kept resurfacing, clawing its way back into my young mind. I didn't know where I should turn. I couldn't tell Grandma; as much as she loved and protected me, she was also a deeply devoted wife. Eventually, I told my mom. I was about eleven or twelve years old, and I remember feeling terrified, unsure if she'd believe me or blame me, or worse. I didn't have the self-possession to know whether I had done something wrong. But instead of the anger I was expecting, Mom's whole face crumpled into an expression of anguish and guilt. She didn't respond, but didn't need to—I could see in her eyes how crushed she felt for not protecting me. I very much doubt that my grandmother ever found out, and I don't even know if Mom told my dad what kind of man his father was and what he had done to me. As far as I know, she kept it to herself. At that time, families especially were dens of silence. And so I learned to compartmentalize. That has been one of several coping mechanisms that has kept the hardships I've faced from overtaking me, but it has not always been the most useful method. Some things in life cannot stay filed away, and the molestation was one of them for me. Even now, when I go to the cemetery—my parents are buried in the same area as my grandparents, just thirteen rows away—I take flowers for Dad, Mom, and Grandma. I avoid even looking at my grandfather's gravesite. Traumas have lasting effects, and they're made so much worse when victims are accused of making it up or exaggerating, or made to feel like their trauma is an unnamable secret and burden they must carry alone. We need to do better. Our baseline for dealing with sexual assault needs to be, *We believe you. I believe you. We will make sure this doesn't happen again.*

Out of all my tragic moments, that sexual assault took the longest—decades, even—to process. It was only upon reflection, especially once I arrived in Washington, that I established that all the confusion and humiliation I'd suppressed had fueled my drive to make sure that predators are held accountable, that victims know that there are people who believe them. I wanted to help others in the way that I needed to be helped. I've experienced the paralysis that follows being violated. I shoved it aside, then feared it was too late to say or do anything, hindered by shame that I was unable to escape the situation or stand up for myself. I relentlessly questioned if it was my fault, if I somehow provoked it, if I should have behaved differently. Self-blaming perpetuates, no matter what age you are. You relive it, relive it, relive it. Even after I reconciled what happened, the cyclical internal debate endured about whether or not to come out with the truth.

My own primitive memory of that time has kept me steadfast in ensuring that victims of sexual abuse receive protection and support. But this is a fight that requires a chorus, and in 2017, I finally heard one when the #MeToo movement galvanized the nation—and I heard it again in 2018 with the Time's Up movement. After the news broke detailing Harvey Weinstein's abuses, an avalanche of revelations about the scale of sexual harassment in American workplaces became public. It was historic; women broke through generations of silence, and we all got to witness a relatively immediate and dynamic shift in accountability. Ever-growing numbers of courageous actors, athletes, comedians, businesswomen, directors, and journalists—from the boardrooms to the breakrooms—stepped forward to share their stories.

I followed the stories from Capitol Hill, the forum with the most microphones and the highest platforms, and nobody around me was saying a word. I had used personal stories as examples and impetus before, and authenticity had always elicited the most powerful responses. Movements originate when the truth is revealed. Since nobody was stepping forward to shine the spotlight into Congress's darkest corners, I did. In late October, I released a video about the chief of staff who had forcibly shoved his tongue in my mouth back when I was a staffer for Leo Ryan. I hoped it would serve as a small but powerful example of the types of obstacles women, especially those coming up in the ranks, face in politics. I wanted that video, which started #MeTooCongress, to assure staffers who were facing similar challenges in the office that they were far from alone, and that that kind of behavior was not okay. I wanted them to feel safe coming to me to share their experiences. I had been there, and I knew what it felt like to carry the burden of that silence. Forty-five years later, I can still remember my own anger and helplessness after that unwanted advance.

Unfortunately, Washington's system has—for years—done a gross disservice to victims. If a victim has wanted to file a complaint, they've had to go to our Office of Congressional Compliance, which Washington created in 1995 to protect itself from being exposed, and it has been remarkably, shamefully successful. Twenty years later, two hundred sixty settlements and more than $15 million have permanently silenced victims of all types of workplace discrimination. In the Office of Compliance, victims are told that they have to spend a month in legal counseling. Then they have to sign a confidentiality agreement and go through a month of mandatory mediation. After that, they are given another month of cooling off. So, for three months, the victims are locked into the terms of that office, while still having to work with their perpetrator. Only after three months of that humiliation can they either settle the case or file an action in court. It's a major deterrent to filing any type of complaint. The harassers remain anonymous and the taxpayers pick up the tab.

After releasing that video, I heard countless gut-wrenching stories. A young, bright woman, filled with potential, sat across from me in my office, sobbing about the abuse she suffered as a congressional employee. Another woman told me how a congressman rubbed up against her and stuck his tongue in her ear, right on the House floor. Yet another staffer was approached by a supervisor, who came up to her desk, unzipped his pants, and pulled out his penis—right in the middle of a work day. A different supervisor dropped two hundred dollars on her desk, stared her down suggestively, and walked away, leaving her in fear. The harassment these women endured was humiliating, but—like the brave servicemembers—they felt more damaged by the broken and unjust complaint process Congress used to protect its own.

In November, I, along with several colleagues, introduced bipartisan legislation to prevent and respond to sexual harassment in Congress and shake up that archaic system. Bills that help protect women from predators should not be a heavy lift, but they have been, historically. Staffers, in particular, are often blackballed for saying anything. One single mother with a young child came to my office, and when I encouraged her to reveal details about the assault she had experienced, told me, "I cannot lose this job." In fear that she certainly would, she has not come forward. She bit her tongue, and nobody has been held accountable. That's just unacceptable. The Member and Employee Training and Oversight On (ME TOO) Congress Act called for more transparency, streamlined the procedure for reporting harassment, and ensured that taxpayers weren't paying for settlements. It stripped away the mandatory nondisclosure agreement and the mediation. The victims would be provided legal counsel, and interns and fellows would be covered by the law as well.

In February 2018, the House passed the Congressional Accountability Reform Act, based on that ME TOO Congress Act. While the act has not been signed into law as I write this, I am confident that this legislation would change the Capitol Hill workplace for the better. It's not often that we're able to pass legislation that directly makes Congress more functional and accountable. I often think back to the Republican committee chairman in 2014 who told me in no uncertain terms that such legislation would never see the light of day. The bill's passing was evidence of progress; it recharged my office and me with hope, and marked the most satisfying legislative victory I've had since being elected to Congress. It was a triumph of bipartisanship, and one that will have a direct impact on every employee who works in our Capitol. There is so much more work to be done. But that first crucial step, coming forward and breaking the silence, has created reverberations that are as deafening as they are gratifying.

While in office, especially during the current administration, I've witnessed the national outrage meter exploding with such force that it's brought us together to say, "No more." So as infuriating as my most recent term of Congress has been, it's also been a profoundly heartening and hopeful time. From all corners of the nation, a new surge of voices is ringing out, demanding that this mishandled power be held responsible, which is precisely what the country needs. Unfortunately, women are still grossly underrepresented in virtually every powerful position—from the C-suites to Congress to the state legislatures. But women are angry. That anger has helped light up civic engagement in a thrilling, palpable way: the number of women seeking elective office is skyrocketing, with thousands filing papers to represent this country, many of whom have never before contemplated running. These are crazy, consequential times, times that in many ways feel like a test of our nation—but Americans' fierce refusal to accept being bullied any longer is changing the tide.

Until we're tested, we have no idea just how much we are capable of achieving. I have been tested, pushed to what I felt certain were my limits, then shoved beyond them, only to discover I am capable of more than I presumed. With the blessing of retrospect, I recognize those moments of losing my footing as the ones that have given me the terrifying freedom to decide who I am and in which direction I will go. I don't know how I would have coped with the tests of the past forty years had it not been for the perspective gained on that dreadful airstrip in Guyana. It very nearly ended my life. Instead, it left me with profound proof that getting out from underneath the wheel, finding the will to stand, and placing one foot in front of the other is the only way to move forward.

A dear friend once told me that each of us is given a task to do in this world. If we don't do it, it won't get done. That's always made a lot of sense to me, as intangible as it may seem. And if there is a task for each of us, I've known for quite some time that mine involves taking action in the service of others. That is my purpose. Every heartbreak and setback, each of the bullets that I've weathered in my life, have only turned me toward a situation that needs reform, or people who need an advocate. And, in spite of all my failures and losses—because of my failures and losses, in fact—I'm not afraid to make noise. And I'm not afraid to fight.

After all, women are tough. We've had to be.

ACKNOWLEDGMENTS

Gratitude has always been an important part of my life. I am so grateful to be alive, to have been given a second chance to live life. So I know gratitude well. Writing this book helped me see my life more clearly. I have learned much more about myself than I knew before. For that I am grateful. Above all, I am most grateful for my parents. I would not have said that before writing this book. I loved my parents completely in life and in death, but I had discounted what a profound effect they had on my life before writing this book. I smugly thought that I had become someone so different from my parents because of my education and experiences. Sheepishly and humbly now, I realize that I am truly a person who grew from them in my values, goals, and achievements. So first and foremost, I thank them.

The greatest accomplishment in my life has been giving birth to my two children, Jackson and Stephanie Sierra. I thank them for occasionally listening to their mom and am endlessly grateful that they have become remarkably committed and talented young adults. I also thank my husband, Barry Dennis, for supporting me through this project, my career, and my life. He has been both a champion and a critic when I needed them the most. A special thank-you goes to my other family members Eric and Laurel Speier, Mary and Bruce Pons, Christy and Nick Dennis, and almost-family Richard and Pat Moomjian and Farro and Sonia Essalat.

I thank Congressman Leo Ryan for recognizing the potential in a young college student. I am also grateful to Congressman and war hero Pete McCloskey who even today—at the age of ninety—provides me with superb counsel and advice.

I thank my cowriter, Domenica Alioto, who helped me put my thoughts on paper and shared late-night edits with enthusiasm. She has become a trusted friend. To Emma Perry, my literary agent, for her sage advice and optimism; and Laura Van der Veer, my editor, who in the midst of planning her wedding was unflappable, enthusiastic, and supportive. I also want to thank the people at Little A and the rest of the production team who helped launch this book: Carmen Johnson, Roni Greenwood, Kamila Forson, Valerie Paquin, Merideth Mulroney, and Emily Freidenrich. I also thank Randi Murray for her longtime belief that this book should be published.

I thank my staff, present and past, who always brought their A game to the difficult task of crafting public policy: Josh Connolly, Richard Steffen, and Mike Thompson, chiefs of staff who have provided me with superior political and legislative expertise throughout my career. Thanks to Brian Perkins, my district director for most of the years I have served in public office, who always had my back, as did Judy Bloom, Susan Bressinden-Smith, Margo Rosen, and Kevin Mullin. Katrina Rill and Mike Larsen have made me sound much smarter than I am in every press release I ever authored and so much more. My outstanding congressional staff, who have been devoted and top notch, deserves a shout out: Tracy Manzer, Miriam Goldstein, Molly Fishman, Mark Nagales, Alexandria Musser, Anne-Marie Boisseau, Sera Alptekin, Estefani Morales, and Mitchel Hochberg. And to former legislative talent, including Elise Thurau, Stacey Dwelley, Erin Ryan, Mandy Smithberger, Tracy Fairchild, Michael Miiller, Susan Wilkinson, Michael Ashcraft, and Melissa Kludjian, who all performed their jobs with superior ability.

One of the great joys in life is the opportunity to keep learning. My decade in Congress has certainly allowed me to "advance" my education in politics, the study of human nature, and what lies behind the curtain. I have learned so much from Nancy Pelosi, whose eye is always on the ball. Dianne Feinstein, who supported me in my run for the State Assembly against political pushback from the power structure, will have my eternal gratitude. I have learned from the great minds and great leaders I serve with, especially John Lewis, Rosa De Lauro, Anna Eshoo, Mike Thompson, George Miller, Sam Farr, Doris Matsui, Paul Tonko, Steny Hoyer, Marcy Kaptur, Louise Slaughter, Rick Nolan, Kathy Castor, Barbara Lee, Jan Schakowsky, John Sarbanes, Lynn Woolsey, Gwen Moore, Carolyn Maloney, Mark DeSaulnier, Jared Huffman, Jerry McNerney, Jim Costa, Frederica Wilson, Beto O'Rourke, David Price, Emanuel Cleaver, John Larson, Jim Cooper, Bob Brady, Lloyd Doggett, Adam Smith, Jim McGovern, Lois Frankel, Annie Kuster, Zoe Lofgren, Mike Honda, Chellie Pingree, Adam Schiff, Jim Himes, Terri Sewell, Andre Carson, Mike Quigley, Joaquin Castro, Denny Heck, Eric Swalwell, Betty McCollum, Lucille Roybal-Allard, Karen Bass, and Grace Napolitano. I have had the good fortune to work with a number of my Republican colleagues on important legislation as well, including Mike McCaul, Bradley Byrne, Walter Jones, Ted Poe, Steve Womack, and Trey Gowdy.

Success in politics is not just passion; it requires not only skill and luck but also great advisors. My career is due in no small part to phenomenal campaign consultants, including David Townsend, the late Bill Cavala, and the late Jim Moore.

I'd like to acknowledge my friends who have really been the wind beneath my wings through all my challenges in life and love, and have made all the difference in the world to me. Kathleen Wentworth, Katy Lawson, Linda Allen, Deborah Stephens, Kari and Dave Foppiano, Adrienne Tissier, Kathy Paulsen, Charlie and Margaret Getz, and Dee O'Moore, who have been my friends for most of my adult life. They have seen it all and still love me! Laura Esserman, Nancy Milliken, Floyd Gonella, Margaret Taylor, Fran Zone, and Joan Cassman became my friends through our professional association, and I'm lucky to have them. My yoga girlfriends always make me laugh: Cynthia Schuman, Christine Krolik, Sheryl Young, Bev Stern, Lilli Rey, Barbara Kaplan, Jennifer Raiser, and Margaret Kramer. The Merry Widows, who have been magnificent soul mates, include Jan Yanehiro, Kathleen Alioto, Sharon Kime, Helen Raiser, Dagmar Dolby, Judy Swanson, Ronnie Caplane, Judy Wilbur, Deborah Strobin, Stacey Case, Debra Dooley, and Jessica McClintock. They have been pillars of strength and support. I thank the Team Jackie Moms from Hillsborough who started out as campaign volunteers and have become wonderful friends who would walk on coals for me . . . and I for them.

So as one can tell, I have much to be grateful for, and I am.

INDEX

J

Z
Zablocki, Clement J., 48

ABOUT THE AUTHOR

Photo © 2018 Steve Maller

Jackie Speier is a California congresswoman. She is a recognized champion of women's rights, privacy, and consumer safety—as well as an avowed opponent of government inefficiency and waste. In 2012, she was named to *Newsweek*'s list of 150 "Fearless Women" in the world and is included in the 2018 "Politico 50" list of top influencers transforming American politics. She is coauthor of *This Is Not the Life I Ordered*. Jackie received a BA in political science from the University of California at Davis, and a JD from UC Hastings College of the Law.

Along with her husband, Barry Dennis; her children, Jackson and Stephanie; and Buddy, their yellow lab, she is a proud fan of the San Francisco Giants and the Golden State Warriors. To learn more about Jackie, visit www.speier.house.gov/about.